De

I dedicate this book to my wife, Jeannette, my children, Lauren and Trey, and grandsons, Karter and Cade. I also dedicate it to my deceased sister and parents.

Dr. Michael L. Bowie, Jr.

I dedicate this book to my beloved wife, Shelley; my children, Detra, Stephen Jr., and Noah; my deceased sister, Mercedes; and parents, William Talbot and Ruth Robinson, who taught me about adaptive, courageous, and intercultural leadership.

Dr. Stephen E. Handy

What Readers are Saying About
DARE TO SHIFT

"In my fifty-plus years of ministry, I have experienced change as a constant. Institutions resist change. The disruption of the covid epidemic has given the church pause to reimagine new possibilities of God. Now is the time for radically new ways of thinking and leading. *Dare to Shift* is a must-read in clearly outlining a path to adaptive leadership for such a time as this."

Mike Slaughter
Passionate Churches, LLC

"Dare to Shift is a summons to every follower of Jesus of Nazareth and every Christian congregation to embrace disruption as an opportunity to claim the habits, practices, and disciplines that will forward the mission of God. Pastors Bowie and Handy have pointed the way with clarity, humility, courage, and grace."

Bishop Gregory V. Palmer
West Ohio Conference of The United Methodist Church

"Drs. Bowie and Handy have extensive experience in cross-cultural, multi-age level, community, civic, small, and large congregation settings. Their shared wisdom in this resource provides insightful teaching and actionable items for leading the church through change and transformation in a post-pandemic season."

Rev. Dr. Rodney T. Smothers
President, RTS Coaching Associates

"You are a leader. You may not be the pastor of a large congregation, CEO of a company, or director of a non-profit, although you might be. No matter your role, this book is for you. Through practical storytelling and scriptural examples, Bowie and Handy invite you to lean into the role God has offered you and grow in the process. Every courageous and curious leader—willing to listen and shift—should take time with this book."

Whitney R. Simpson
Author, Spiritual Director, and Retreat Leader

"Dare to Shift is a post-pandemic, permission-giving, practical book filled with two highly effective leaders' combined knowledge, wisdom, and ministry experiences. This book by Dr. Bowie and Dr. Handy is an invitation to shift in a new direction, experiencing fun and fruitfulness in ministry again."

Dr. Candace M Lewis
President/Dean Gammon Theological Seminary

"Now and then, a fresh approach to Discipleship and Leadership emerges. *Dare to Shift* captures, in a compelling way, the challenge to engage the culture with innovation by becoming entrepreneurial as disciples of Jesus.

- Now is the time.
- Before you is the road map.
- Time is short.

Grab a group of leaders, dive into Dare to Shift, and see what God will do in your context."

Bishop Bill McAlilly
Tennessee-Western Kentucky Conference, The United Methodist Church

"Leadership at this moment requires a new paradigm shift responsive to a new way of engagement that allows the mission to be relevant. Dr. Bowie and Dr. Handy challenge us to be innovative thinkers and prophetic leaders who are self-aware of how to show up and align creatively. Their holistic approach provides transformation and not transactional learning, useful nuggets, personal and collective reflection opportunities, and hope for a new era of leadership willing to pivot and do it differently."

Rev. Dr. Giovanni Arroyo
General Secretary, General Commission on Religion and Race
The United Methodist Church

"Leadership requires adaptability. To solve the complex problems we face, we must listen to all stakeholders, consider all implications of the possible solutions, and most importantly, be willing to pivot, recognizing that solutions, just like problems, are organic in nature. This book gives you practical tools to shift your mindset and prepare for major shifts in your organization."

Sedrik Newbern
Author, Professor, and Business Consultant

"It is easy to discuss the need for change philosophically. Still, it is quite another thing to actually make the necessary SHIFTS in our lives personally, emotionally, vocationally, and spiritually required to survive the turbulence normalized in our post-pandemic world. Dr. Bowie is one of my dearest friends, and I have witnessed him live the words of this book in ways that will help us all prepare for what is vital in this next iteration of ministry."

Dr. Rudy Rasmus
Co-Founder/Executive Director, Bread of Life Inc. Houston

DARE TO SHIFT

Challenging leaders to a new way of thinking

Dr. Michael Bowie & Dr. Stephen Handy

Foreword by Bishop Tracy Smith Malone

Market Square
BOOKS

Dare to Shift

Challenging leaders to a new way of thinking

©2023 Market Square Publishing, LLC

books@marketsquarebooks.com
141 N. Martinwood, Suite 20   Knoxville, Tennessee 37923

ISBN: 978-1-950899-71-5

Printed and Bound in the United States of America
Cover Illustration & Book Design ©2023 Market Square Publishing, LLC

Foreword: Bishop Tracy Smith Malone
Editor: Sheri Carder Hood
Post-Process Editor: Ken Rochelle
Page Design: Carrie Rood
Cover Design: Kevin Slimp

All rights reserved. No part of this book may be reproduced in any manner without written permission except in the case of brief quotations included in critical articles and reviews. For information, please contact Market Square Publishing, LLC.

Scripture quotations used with permission from:

CEB
Scripture quotations from the COMMON ENGLISH BIBLE. © Copyright 2011 COMMON ENGLISH BIBLE. All rights reserved. Used by permission. (www.CommonEnglishBible.com).

NRSV
New Revised Standard Version Bible, copyright © 1989 National Council of the Churches of Christ in the United States of America. Used by permission. All rights reserved worldwide.

NIV
Scriptures marked NIV are taken from the NEW INTERNATIONAL VERSION (NIV): Scripture taken from THE HOLY BIBLE, NEW INTERNATIONAL VERSION ®. Copyright© 1973, 1978, 1984, 2011 by Biblica, Inc.™. Used by permission of Zondervan.

Contents

Foreword 1
Bishop Bishop Tracy Smith Malone

Preface 5
Dare to Shift

Chapter One 7
Reoriented Thinking & Shifting Mindset

Chapter Two 29
Renewing Fellowship

Chapter Three 51
Reevaluating Leadership

Chapter Four 77
Rethinking Entrepreneurship

Chapter Five 95
Realigning Relationships

Chapter Six 113
Reevaluating Stewardship

Chapter Seven 139
Recapturing/Reclaiming Discipleship

Chapter Eight 157
Reinvesting in Cultures of Experimentation

Concluding Integration 173

FOREWORD

Bishop Tracy Smith Malone

I have been in ministry for over 30 years and have served in various leadership positions at every church level. Throughout these years, I have coached many people of all ages to help them expand their leadership capacity, achieve their leadership goals, and to help them flourish in their work and lives. I have discovered that people who desire to become effective and influential leaders have demonstrated that they are teachable, adaptive, and resilient. They are leaders who have learned and recognize that their greatest leadership potential is more fully realized in their personal willingness to expand their imagination and embrace change.

The Church needs Christ-centered leaders, lay and clergy, prepared and equipped to lead in places and communities and among people plagued with trauma, chaos, and fear. The Church needs Christ-centered leaders who have the courage and commitment to assess and address the current realities of the landscape of their ministry context (or mission field) and who are bold in taking the necessary steps that lead toward transformation and healing. And the Church needs Christ-centered leaders who are motivated to inspire hope and unity and to empower others to join in the work for peace, justice, and the building of God's Beloved Community.

Dr. Michael Bowie and Dr. Stephen Handy are strong examples of Christ-centered leadership. I have known both of these pastoral leaders for many years and have served with them in various contexts within the life of the Church. I first met Dr. Handy when we served on the General Commission on Religion and Race (GCORR). I remember being impressed by his passion for equity and inclusion and his heart for developing leaders in his local church as he was leading them into becoming a multi-cultural/multi-ethnic congregation. I remember meeting Dr. Bowie at the National Black Methodists for Church Renewal (BMCR) annual meeting. I grew to know him personally when we participated in conversations regarding the future of The United Methodist Church. I remember being impressed by his prophetic vision of a Church where everyone belonged and had a seat at the table.

In their respective ministries, I have witnessed how

Dr. Bowie and Dr. Handy have transformed people's lives and impacted communities. I have seen their commitment to self-care and professional development by attending to their renewal and continuing education. I have observed how they have dedicated themselves to equipping leaders for greater discipleship, social witness, and living their best lives. I am encouraged by their passionate desire to challenge the Church – lay and clergy – with new ways of thinking about leadership and ministry in these present times and amid the many current realities. And as a result of my appreciation for who they are and how they lead, I have utilized their skills, gifts, and expertise in my leadership roles and work.

Dare to Shift is a thought-provoking, experiential leadership book full of insights and wisdom for leaders (lay and clergy) who want to level up their capacity to lead more effectively. It is a book for leaders ready to shift their leadership paradigm and discover something new and different about themselves and their leadership capacity.

Dr. Bowie and Dr. Handy share some of their learnings from their in-depth leadership experiences and provide strategies and practical steps that assist leaders in doing the necessary work of "mindset shifting" for new ways of leading. They invite leaders to disrupt their own complacency and fear and embrace a bold, prophetic, and risk-taking way of doing ministry.

What is helpful and what I appreciate about this book is that each chapter introduces a different concept and practice for "right side" leadership. They are grounded in scripture and biblical principles. At the conclusion of each chapter, questions are provided to invite the reader into deeper reflection. Not only will readers learn about what it means to be a transformational leader, but readers will also engage in the study of scripture and theological reflection.

I am inspired by this book's passionate teachings, examples of leadership, and the challenge, inspiration, and hope it offers. I am encouraged by the gift it will be to individual readers and leaders who will read and study it together and imagine the difference it will make in their churches, communities, and personal lives.

As you read this book, may you be encouraged to "shift" and to think in new and radical ways about your leadership.

Tracy Smith Malone
Bishop, The United Methodist Church

PREFACE
Dare to Shift

For nearly three years, the world has experienced a disruption that changed life as we knew it. This disruption has forced us to shift in every area of life. Friends, nothing will ever be the same. How we shop, work, and even worship has forever changed. Let's be honest. A major shift has happened!

In this book, we will discuss how the Resurrection of Jesus caused the ultimate disruption to life, changing the landscape of the world for all time. In John 21:1-12, the resurrected Jesus appears to the disciples after their unsuccessful night of fishing. Not realizing the meaning or magnitude of the Resurrection, the disciples did not immediately adapt to the new reality. They continued to fish as they were accustomed. The disciples were so stuck on how they used to catch fish that they did not *shift*. Instead, they did the same thing *all night* and caught nothing! With direction from Jesus, the disciples eventually realized that the Resurrection impacted their lives **personally, emotionally, vocationally, and spiritually.**

Friends, adaptive leadership is vital for this next iteration of ministry. To be effective, we must be nimble, flexible, and open to new ways of ministry. We can no longer rely on how we've always done things. We must be willing to *shift* and do ministry in uncommon, uncertain, and uncomfortable ways.

As society continues to navigate and adjust to this new reality, we need to transform our complacent mindset into a creative one. This book will challenge you to make intentional shifts in your understanding of relationships, leadership, stewardship, and discipleship. We also hope you will feel encouraged to embrace new models and concepts compelling you to be more curious, creative, and courageous.

We urge you to read this book, embody each chapter and make the needed shift to experience the abundant life you were meant to live. We encourage you to move beyond an ordinary life of routine and comfort. **We dare you to shift!**

Dr. Michael Bowie
Strengthening the Black Church for the 21st Century (SBC21)
National Executive Director of SBC21

Dr. Stephen Handy
McKendree United Methodist Church
Lead Pastor
Director of Urban Cohort

CHAPTER ONE

Reoriented Thinking & Shifting Mindset

By Mike Bowie

The renewed mind is the Canvass in which the Spirit of God can paint.

Bill Johnson

On March 13, 2020, we experienced a disruption that will never be forgotten. I was in Nashville, Tennessee, for a board meeting, and at 7:38 a.m., I was watching the local news as our world shut down. According to reporters, a virus originating in Asia was covering America like a blanket. Until this point, the world hadn't experienced a disruption of this proportion since the yellow fever virus.

My heart rate increased, and I began to sweat profusely as the news reported that the March Madness NCAA basketball tournament and all Broadway shows had been canceled. Several thoughts consumed my mind, and none of them made sense. It felt like the world was coming to an end. I remember reading the front cover of *Time* magazine: "What to Know and What to Do About the Global Pandemic" and how to keep your family safe at home. It was just another reminder of how this horrific pandemic had disrupted life as we'd known it.

But this wasn't the first time the world experienced a disruption. I daresay the Resurrection of Jesus Christ provided the ultimate disruption that changed the world for good and marked the beginning of an emerging, new kingdom.

Unlike the Roman Empire, which Caesar Augustus ruled through intimidation, hate, and fear, the Kingdom of God was driven by compassion, justice, and love for all people. The Kingdom of God was a visible demonstration on Earth of an invisible reality in heaven. God's goal was—and is—for God's will to be done on Earth through his son, Jesus, just as it is in heaven. With this understanding, the life, death, and resurrection of Jesus effectively introduced a new kingdom, a countercultural model for living that contrasted the rule of the Roman Empire.

Jesus' Challenge: A New Way of Thinking

In this new community, people participated in life together and had all things in common. Living into this new movement called "The Way" required a reorientation of thinking, a shifting of one's mindset. For years, the disciples had been accustomed to living under the rules of the Roman Empire, but Jesus challenged the disciples to alter their thinking to be kingdom-centered. As Jesus reminded them in one of his longest sermons, the Sermon on the Mount, Matthew 6:33: "Instead, desire first and foremost God's kingdom and God's righteousness, and all these things will be given to you as well" (CEB).

The disciples were committed to physically following Jesus, but they still needed to be transformed in their minds. As we are told in Romans 12:2, "Don't be conformed to the patterns of this world but be transformed by the renewing of your minds" (CEB). To be fully devoted to following Jesus requires a surrendering of the will—the flesh. It requires a conversation of the heart and a renewal or reorientation of the mind.

Throughout Jesus' thirty-three years of ministry, he taught about this kingdom and demonstrated its countercultural lifestyle. Not only did he introduce a new way of living to the disciples, but on several occasions, Jesus also gave them a forewarning about his death. The disciples heard Jesus' words as he told them exactly what was going to happen, but they, unfortunately, did not fully understand what he meant.

> *"The Son of Man is going to be delivered into the hands of men. They will kill him, and after three days he will rise." But they did not understand what he meant and were afraid to ask him about it.*
>
> **Mark 9:31-32 (NIV)**

Because of the disciples' fear and unwillingness to clarify Jesus' words, upon Jesus' death, they found themselves grief-stricken, lost, and confused. They did not comprehend that three days after his crucifixion, Jesus would rise again. Even though the disciples watched Jesus die on the cross on Good Friday, they either didn't believe or remember that he would be resurrected early Sunday morning. When Mary, Mary Magdalene, and the other women returned to the tomb, to their surprise, the stone had already been rolled away. After summoning Peter and the other disciples, they walked into an empty tomb and saw strips of linen and a cloth that had been wrapped around Jesus' head—but Jesus wasn't there.

Now, you would think that after seeing the empty tomb, the disciples would have had an epiphany and remembered Jesus' words before his death telling them that he would rise again in three days. But they didn't.

How often are we just like the disciples? Jesus gives us a promise of healing. We confess with our mouths, but in our minds, we don't fully comprehend or believe.

Addressing the Trauma

To be honest, numerous times in my life, I've been in overwhelming predicaments and said, "I believe," but I didn't know how the situation would turn out. It reminds me of the father in Mark 9:24, who cried out to Jesus to heal his son, confessing that he believed but begging Jesus to help his unbelief. Today, even in our unbelief, Jesus will always extend grace and give us another opportunity to believe. Isn't that good news? Even when we fall short or miss the mark, grace gives us another chance to get it right.

After his death, Jesus appeared to the disciples early in the morning while they were fishing. Now, these men were professional fishermen, and after they had fished all night, Jesus appeared on the shore and asked them if they had caught any fish. The disciples didn't recognize his face or his voice.

Could it have been the time of day, or was the Resurrection a major disruption that altered the disciples' vision, for it was only a few days earlier that they had sat at the foot of the cross and watched Jesus bleed profusely and die an agonizing death? As they heard Jesus cry out those seven last words and watched his traumatic death on the cross, I imagine it was like brother George Perry Floyd crying out for his mother, declaring, "I can't breathe!"

If I may take some liberty with this text, I contend that these disciples were suffering from Post-Traumatic Crucifixion Syndrome. They didn't realize the impact this public lynching of their friend and teacher had on their psyche. Such a traumatic event should have compelled them to seek professional help, but instead, the disciples went back to business as usual.

Friends, there's a real danger in ignoring the trauma that the global pandemic caused within us. Instead of seeking professional help, many of us—like the disciples—have forged through and continue to do business as usual. Yet research shows that this major disruption has negatively impacted the emotional well-being of 59 percent of clergy and 56 percent of laity.

The disciples were unwilling or unable to make a mental shift during the disruption, determined to fish and do life the same way as before. They were so accustomed to doing business as usual that they didn't have the mental wherewithal to realize the way they were fishing was no longer effective. The life, death, and resurrection of Jesus changed everything!

Now, let's be honest: Doing ministry on the left side BC (Before COVID) worked, and you could routinely do ministry without much innovation, courage, or creativity. Ministry just, well, happened. See, on the left side, things were certain, common, and comfortable. But the Resurrection forced the disciples to shift from the left side to the right. The disciples would soon discover that things are uncertain, unconventional, and uncomfortable on the right side, and one cannot predict what will happen. On the right side, you can expect new things to happen, but there will be times when you must get comfortable with being uncomfortable and wait. And remember, as we wait on the Lord, we are not idly waiting with crossed fingers. Rather, we are waiting *in* the Lord with an open heart of great expectancy, knowing that the amazing catch will come. We don't know when, but it will come to pass.

The disciples needed to develop the courage to adapt and transition from fishing on the left side to the right side. Let me be clear—the "right side" is not a political position or ideology but a new, countercultural, creative way of living. Jesus literally instructed his disciples to cast their nets from the right side of the boat rather than the left side: **"Cast the net on the right side of the boat, and you will find some"** (John 21:6 ESV).

I contend that this new right-side reality was the mental shift needed for the disciples to live in the Kingdom of God effectively. Therefore, this new approach to living on the right side should be paramount and evident in all we do today, from what we purchase to what we wear. Our words and behavior should reflect this right-side reality. When Jesus said in Mathew 6:33 to seek him first, he was explaining to the disciples that this seeking required an intentional, right-side reorientation of their thinking.

A Courageous Shift

As the world shifts out of this disruption, we must courageously embrace a right-side mindset to help us navigate through uncertain, unconventional, and uncomfortable seasons. Know that adopting this new mindset will not be easy, but it will be worth it. There will be some behaviors, practices, and people that need to be released. To effectively live into this new reality, our control, complacency, and complaining must be surrendered. We must get uncomfortable and release persons who are toxic and taint our dreams. We must be willing to let go of the limitation and scarcity thinking that affects our generosity and abundant living.

I have struggled with this mindset mostly when I think I'm not good enough or deserving. However, I discovered one day that my thinking and mindset had nothing to do with God's grace and mercy toward me.

To anyone reading this chapter, remember: God will use your past disappointments as preparation for your future destiny. Now, I know that sounds cliché, but the disciples soon discovered that, even though they experienced a mess on the left side, there was a miracle waiting on the right side for them and their friends.

All it took was one shift.

Could you be one shift away from your miracle, your breakthrough? Although this sounds simple, it can be very challenging when you possess a fixed mindset. Psychologist Carol Dweck, known for her work and research on motivation and mindset, says a "fixed mindset" is when a person believes their personal qualities, such as intelligence and personality, are innate and unchangeable.[1] Many of us are trained in this fixed mindset from an early age. When we cling to a fixed mindset, it's nearly impossible to experience the brand-new thing God has in store for us. Especially during this season of uncertainty, we must shift from a fixed mindset to a growth mindset. In a growth mindset, people can change and improve. With a growth mindset, you believe the abilities you're born with are only a starting point. You possess a passion for learning, welcome mistakes as opportunities to grow, and seek challenges to push yourself. A growth mindset occurs when you are open to learning and experiencing new

---

[1] https://www.edglossary.org./growth-mindset/.

things. Cultivating a growth mindset is invaluable to ensure you can shift your thinking.

My Personal Tiberias

Now, the location where the disciples chose to fish was called the Sea of Tiberias. *Tiberias* means "man's lowest point," and perhaps it was not coincidental that they were now in a place where their lives were at their lowest pont. Before Jesus and the Resurrection, life and all they knew happened on the left side. Life on the left side of the boat was metaphorically common, certain, and comfortable, with relatively routine daily events and little surprise. This life, of course, was also relatively mundane and not as adventuresome.

As I thought about this, it reminded me of my lowest point, my personal Tiberias, back in January 2008. I was the teaching pastor at Ginghamsburg Church, a United Methodist congregation in Tipp City, Ohio. It was a gray, windy Tuesday, and I was giving a report when I began stuttering uncontrollably and then lost consciousness. The next thing I knew, I was on a Life Flight to Miami Valley Hospital. Now, if memory serves me correctly, passengers who need Life Flight are either dead or about to expire. Thankfully for me, it was the latter.

I wasn't aware that, for twelve years, I had been

growing a meningioma tumor on the right frontal lobe of my brain. As the radiologist scanned my brain, they discovered a baseball-size tumor. Although it was an abnormal growth, the good news was it was benign and on the right side. But I can truly say, in my "Tiberias," that tumor disrupted my entire life and reoriented my thinking. For six months, I went through intense speech and physical therapy.

All in all, I was at one of the lowest points of my life, in that proverbial boat in my personal Sea of Tiberias. During this season of uncertainty, I didn't know if my life was coming to an end.

Maybe you have experienced something similar. Perhaps there are moments in your life when you find yourself doing well, then unexpectedly, you experience your own Tiberias, possibly a matter of life or death.

At that moment, the lowest point of your life, you may not realize something greater will come out of your Tiberias.

Looking back, I now realize that when the world experienced that unexpected COVID-19 disruption in March 2020, I didn't get too anxious because I had been there before. I knew the same God who was with me while I was being life-flighted, the same God who was with me when the baseball-sized tumor was removed, the same God who was with me when I battled many days wondering if it was over for me was the very same God who would be with us through the pandemic.

Every day, I stood on Isaiah 54:17, that no weapon formed against me should prosper. And every day, I declared the psalmist's boldness: "I shall not die, but live and declare the works of the Lord" (Psalm 118:17 KJV). These two promises reoriented my thinking, helping me realize that every disruption impacting our lives is just an incubator giving birth to a brand-new possibility. The bottom line is that if God were with me when a baseball-sized tumor in my brain disrupted my life, surely God would be with me during the disruption of COVID-19.

With this shift in my thinking, I have been gifted with the ability to view any problem as a possibility. I can see every burden as a blessing and look at every mishap as a miracle in the making. Okay, I'm not trying to sneak a preach, but you get the point!

When we reorient and shift our thinking, it changes our perspective. Dr. Joe Dispenza, an international lecturer and researcher on rewiring the human brain for self-healing, says that where our attention goes, the energy flows. That is, we must think with intentionality. For example, you can drive past your favorite restaurant, and before you know it, you are hungry. Where you focus is where your attention will usually manifest.

Disruption for the Adventure

Friends, if you wish to experience the brand-new life waiting on the right side, you must shift your mindset and stop dwelling on your problems. Instead, shift your focus to the possibilities of God. Don't focus on your obstacles. Focus on your opportunities. Don't focus on your budget, but focus on building the Kingdom of God. Remember: where our attention goes, the energy flows.

So, let's be honest. What consumes most of your attention? Is it a toxic relationship, a dead-end career, or financial difficulties?

Dr. Handy and I pray you allow the power of the Holy Spirit to reorient your thinking to a "right-side" perspective so that you can see this disruption as a blessing, and not a burden. This isn't prosperity jargon, some sort of name-it-and-claim-it rhetoric, but rather the Word of God as manifested in Romans 8:28: "And we know that all things work together for good to those who love God, to those who are the called according to His purpose" (NKJV).

The last three years may have been difficult, but somehow God will use this disruption for our good! I believe the Apostle Paul reminds us that whenever we find ourselves in our own Sea of Tiberias, we must shift our thinking and be deliberate with the words that come out of our mouths. We can give thanks in our situation, or we can complain.

In his article entitled "Complaining Only Makes Things Worse," Dr. Dale Robbins writes:

> *I used to think people complained because they had a lot of problems. But I have come to realize that many have problems because they complain. An attitude of grumbling, griping, murmuring, squawking doesn't change anything or make situations better.*[2]

Complaining steals your peace, kills your joy, and robs your hope. When you find yourself stuck in your Sea of Tiberias, shift your thinking, change your language, and don't complain. Instead, continue to give God thanks—because, like my brain tumor, the bigger the burden, the bigger the blessing.

I'm convinced, like never before, that God uses our Tiberias moments to prepare us so we can experience right-side living. In other words, God allows us to be disrupted so we can begin to live adventures—and adventures are almost always unpredictable and uncomfortable. With that understanding, we must not settle by going back to normal, predictable, left-side living. If we have learned anything from this disruptive season, it is that normal living, left-side living is antiquated, outdated, and obsolete. I saw a T-shirt that

---

[2] https://www.victorious.org/pub/how-become-christian-182.

summed it up best: "Normal is not coming back, but Jesus is!" So, I encourage you to stop looking for normal. Alter your language and raise the level of your expectancy.

During this season of disruption, God is challenging followers of Jesus to seek right-side living, which calls for courage, boldness, and risk-taking—that is, it calls for faith. Hebrews 11:1 tells us that "faith is the substance of things hoped for, the evidence of things not seen" (NKJV). I contend that everything we do requires risk-taking and faith. The Apostle Paul reminds us that without risk-taking, it's impossible to please God. Faith is vital for leaders to experience the amazing things God has for us—in our families, in our relationships, and even in our careers. In this same way, Jesus encouraged the disciples to shift their perspectives, change how they worked, and take a risk. Friends, I pray you don't miss your breakthrough because you aren't willing to get uncomfortable, reorient and shift your thinking, or settle for your old ways.

The disciples were so accustomed to living with a left-side mindset that when the Resurrection disrupted their lives, they had to make a choice: continue to seek common, usual, and normal living or shift to uncommon, unpredictable, and unusual living. Right now, you also must make a choice and take a risk. How long will you continue to accept a left-side life where it's just enough? Or will you shift to the right side to experience a life of more than enough?

Fishing on the Right

When I think about living uncommonly, uncertainly, and uncomfortably, I remember three months before the pandemic, I heard the Holy Spirit telling me to get ready to shift and take a risk. I didn't know that in July 2020, I was about to experience a vocational disruption that would shift me from being a senior pastor for more than twenty years in the local church to being a national executive director responsible for providing resources to more than two thousand Black churches.

When I arrived on the job as the new national executive director of Strengthening the Black Church for the 21st Century (SBC21), I found I needed to reorient my thinking immediately. I was forced to make a drastic mental shift because this was a different kind of ministry—and one with a global platform. No longer solely responsible for one congregation, as the national director of SBC21, I'm responsible for providing relevant, cutting-edge, innovative resources to strengthen congregations and transform communities. Now, I must admit the mental shift wasn't as challenging as it initially appeared because I realized that God had been preparing me for this position since the beginning of my ordained ministry as an elder in 1998.

I contend that my denomination, the United Methodist Church, has been operating with a left-side mindset and expecting right-side results. Since the 1968 merger between The Methodist Church and the Evangelical United Brethren Church into the United Methodist Church, this newly formed denomination has been driven by privilege, proceeds, and power. The United Methodist Church has been a blessing to me, but I must confess, it hasn't come without consternation, irritation, and frustration.

When I began my journey toward ordained ministry in 1993 at St. John's Downtown in Houston, Texas, under the leadership of then-pastors Rudy and Juanita Rasmus, its missional focus was on the least, last, and lost. Every week, I witnessed how the homeless, chemically addicted, and HIV-infected were all treated with unconditional love and as persons of profound value and dignity. Matthew 25:35-36 (NIV) sums up this ministry:

> *For I was hungry and you gave me something to eat, I was thirsty and you gave me something to drink, I was a stranger and you invited me in, I needed clothes and you clothed me, I was sick and you looked after me, I was in prison and you came to visit me.*

As I reflect on this Scripture, I realize that for more than thirty years, St. John's has been operating on the right side, and God has been accomplishing amazing things through this church in the heart of downtown Houston. I also realize that I have been operating from this right-side mindset too. It was at St. John's Church that God reoriented my thinking from a desire to attend law school to attending seminary. Since my time there twenty-five years ago, I have developed some unconventional ministry concepts, made risky decisions, and served in uncomfortable appointments. Looking back, it's as if my entire ministry has been done with a right-side mindset in a denomination stuck with a left-side mentality.

However, prior to transitioning into this new role, the United Methodist Church experienced a huge disruption in February 2019 at the Special Session of the General Conference in St. Louis, Missouri. Shortly after the decision was made, I recall writing a letter to Saint Luke Community UMC as their Sr. Pastor, with an update and my thoughts:

Dear St. Luke family,

I greet you in the strong and liberating name of Jesus Christ! Many of you know that I attended the special-called General Conference #GC2019 in St. Louis, Missouri from Feb. 23-26 to address the issue of same-sex marriage and ordination of homosexuals. I would like to give you a brief update on the final decision and the future way forward for the UMC.

After much deliberation and debating, the General Conference approved the Traditional Plan, which maintains the existing prohibitions and enforces more stringent penalties. The Traditional Plan passed by a vote of 438 to 384. To my amazement, the One Church model failed by the same margin, which is a clear indication that the UMC is divided on this issue. The entire Traditional Plan will be reviewed by the Judicial Council (the Supreme Court) to determine if it's constitutional.

When the final decision was made on Feb 26, it was as if we were reliving 1787 when Absalom Jones and Richard Allen were reminded that they could not kneel and pray in St. George's Methodist Church in Philadelphia. Even though they were gifted preachers and leaders, they still weren't fully accepted into the community. Unfortunately, for far too long, many people have merely been tolerated and not truly celebrated in the UMC.

Since the inception of the UMC in 1968, people of color, women and the LGBTQ community have been tolerated and not fully accepted or celebrated. As an ordained elder for over twenty years, I want to personally apologize to all the LGBTQ community and other advocates for justice who may have felt like #GC2019 was equivalent to 1787. But during my time of reflection, I've realized that there's no legislation, amendments, or votes that can determine a person's worth, value, and dignity in the Kingdom of God!

I believe that ordained elders have a responsibility to make sure that everyone is included in the Beloved Community. So what does that mean for St. Luke? As a congregation, we will abide by the Book of Discipline, but we will continue to intentionally love, celebrate, and embrace all of God's people. If you have other questions regarding the #GC2019 decision made, please don't hesitate to schedule an appointment with me @ 214 887.3903. Even though many of us are still disappointed by the decision, be encouraged. The Apostle Paul reminds us in 1 Thessalonians 5:17 to rejoice always, pray continually, and give thanks because God isn't through with us yet!

Embrace life,
Pastor Bowie

You may ask, what does this have to do with reorientating and shifting your thinking? I contend that we fail to see that, before COVID-19, the United Methodist Church was operating on the left side for at least fifty-plus years—or, I daresay, since 1844. As I mentioned in my letter, the final decision on February 26, 2019, felt as if we were reliving the oppression of all those years ago, in 1787, when Absalom Jones and Richard Allen were told they could not kneel and pray in St. George's Methodist Church in Philadelphia. It felt like all those years when people of color, women, and the LGBTQI community were merely tolerated, not fully accepted or celebrated.

When we in the United Methodist Church experienced the 2019 disruption in St. Louis at the Special Session of the General Conference, like the disciples, we continued to do ministry as usual on the left side. Unfortunately, a year later, we experienced the larger disruption of COVID-19, and now the denomination is on the verge of separation.

Providentially, it took a global disruption to force my denomination to do ministry in cutting-edge, creative, and innovative ways, and I'm sure that's true of most denominations. Leaders were forced to reorient their thinking to experience the awesome things still happening in the "Sea of Tiberias."

As I write this chapter, some congregations have chosen to disaffiliate and leave the United Methodist Church. But I'm convinced that a right-side shift has happened, and God is doing something brand new.

Questions for Reflection

1. Can you think of a time when you experienced your own "Sea of Tiberias" or a major life disruption that caused you to question your own faith and relationship with God?

2. As you reflect on difficult times, do you feel those experiences brought you closer to God or distanced you from God?

3. In your daily life, do you find yourself focusing on problems or possibilities?

CHAPTER TWO

Renewing Fellowship

By Mike Bowie

Alone, we can do so little; together, we can do so much.

Helen Keller

After the Resurrection, Peter chose to go fishing. We don't know if it was for pleasure or his profession. Whatever the purpose, he chose to fish in the same manner he was accustomed to, and the other disciples did too. Despite the disruption of the Resurrection, they continued to operate business as usual.

I see the same today. After we experience any form of disruption in life, it's often tempting to default back to what we are familiar with and comfortable doing. But as the T-shirt I mentioned said, "Normal is never coming back, but Jesus is!" This sums up our new reality.

Now back to the disciples. You seldom find the disciples fishing or participating in public activities individually.

Their lives were rooted in a deep sense of fellowship and communion. Fellowship was a common trait in the disciples' way of living. The purpose of fellowship wasn't simply to hang out and be together. Rather, it was to experience koinonia. "Koinonia" refers to the fellowship of sharing the love of Christ in community. A New Testament concept, koinonia describes the depth of belonging to the Christian community. It was the original right-side experience where things were uncertain, uncommon, and uncomfortable.

"Koinonia" is also translated as "communion." The same love that God lavished on the disciples through the person of Jesus Christ was the same love they shared with one another in community. This love for Jesus compelled them to live countercultural lives with one another as demonstrated in Acts 2.

Why Koinonia?

On several occasions throughout the New Testament, we witness the importance of Jesus' followers being together in fellowship, or koinonia. When they met together daily, they developed a deeper level of intimacy and communion. They realized koinonia was cultivated in community, not in isolation. Acts 2:42-47 (NIV) exemplifies this fellowship and community with other believers:

They devoted themselves to the apostles' teaching and to fellowship, to the breaking of bread and to prayer. Everyone was filled with awe at the many wonders and signs performed by the apostles. All the believers were together and had everything in common. They sold property and possessions to give to anyone who had need. Every day they continued to meet together in the temple courts. They broke bread in their homes and ate together with glad and sincere hearts, praising God and enjoying the favor of all the people. And the Lord added to their number daily those who were being saved.

The Book of Acts highlights several essential elements of Christian fellowship and koinonia:

- Studying apostle teachings
- Breaking bread and sharing a meal
- Possessing a common mission and purpose
- Being concerned about others' needs
- Being connected to a multicultural community and experiencing consistent growth for the expansion of the new movement.

Therefore, we see how being in fellowship/koinonia with one another was an opportunity to engage with other people and create a sacred place to experience God. Because of their intentionality to live in koinonia, God equipped and empowered all who were present with the power of the Holy Spirit. As we study this Acts 2 community model of fellowship/koinonia, we must ask the question: Where did this power to live together come from?

In Acts 1:8, Jesus encouraged the disciples to stay together in Jerusalem in the Upper Room until they received this power, and in Acts 2:1-4 (CEB), his promise came to pass:

> *When Pentecost Day arrived, they were all together in one place. Suddenly a sound from heaven like the howling of a fierce wind filled the entire house where they were sitting. They saw what seemed to be individual flames of fire alighting on each one of them. They were all filled with the Holy Spirit and began to speak in other languages as the Spirit enabled them to speak.*

Friends, this passage is a great reminder of what happens when people from all nations and races are together in accord: amazing things happen! So why do we need Diversity, Equity, and Inclusion (DEI) Training? It's because unity was God's original plan for humanity. The day of Pentecost was not only the birth of the Church, but it was also a moment to be empowered to love God and to love and serve people. Pentecost is a great reminder that God does amazing things when people are together in one accord and share a common mission. With this understanding of the power of koinonia, dysfunctional families can be revived, blighted communities can be renewed, and even a divided Congress can be restored—if only there is a sense of togetherness and harmony.

A Christ-centered Agenda

As I write this chapter, the midterm elections results are in. The Republicans now control the House, and the Democrats control the Senate, illustrating the continued divisions in our country. But we must never forget that ultimate power belongs to God. Psalm 24:1 (CEB) reminds us, "The earth is the Lord's and everything in it, the world and its inhabitants, too."

During this chaotic and crazy time, we must remember that infinite power is not determined by what occurs on Capitol Hill. That revelation was made more than two thousand years ago on Calvary's Hill. I also contend that many of the problems facing America today—poverty, homelessness, and mass incarceration—have more to do with humanity, ego, and surrendering to God's ultimate sovereignty, authority, and will.

On the day of Pentecost, the disciples needed spiritual power to live counterculturally that ultimately changed the trajectory of the world. The power of the Holy Spirit equipped the disciples to participate in a new movement called The Way. Being a part of this movement wasn't popular, and they immediately became a target of mockery, ridicule, and even persecution. And despite all the challenges they encountered, they were still expected to share the good news of the Gospel and make disciples for Jesus Christ for the transformation of the world. Now, think about that for a second. Every day, they sought to live in community as Jesus taught them. For instance, if someone slaps you on your right cheek, you must turn the left cheek to them as well (Matthew 5:38).

Yet today, we live in a time when you can lose your life if you accidentally cut someone off in traffic or unknowingly take their parking spot. Friends, I believe the answer to gun violence and road rage is not more legislation, mass incarceration, but sanctification. Sanctification according to Book of Discipline (Resource UMC) is the continuing process of being made perfect in love and of removing the desire to sin. Therefore, we don't need a new committee, a special conference, but we need the power of the Holy Spirit to become people of love.

With that understanding, in the context of koinonia, people gather to discuss and share the hell they experienced last week but know that God will give us power next week to show others how awesome God is. Unfortunately, we live in a period where people struggle every day to decide whether Jesus or Ralph Lauren is Lord. What Lord seeks your allegiance daily?

As I think about this question of allegiance, I realize how tiring our journey can be and how much effort it takes to live as a dual citizen of both heaven and earth. The late Dr. Myles Munroe said it this way:

> *All kingdom citizens carry dual citizenship, where citizens of a country may hold simultaneously legal citizenship in another. Children born to citizens of one country who are living in another country generally become citizens of both countries.*
>
> *It is no different with the Kingdom of Heaven. All kingdom citizens are simultaneously citizens of the Kingdom of Heaven as well as citizens of the earthly nation of their birth or their naturalization. We don't give up our earthly citizenship when we become citizens of the kingdom. And in the same way, we don't have to be in heaven to benefit from heavenly jurisdiction. Our citizenship is constant, and the kingdom government exercises jurisdiction over us wherever we are.*[3]

Even though we are merely human, we are expected to walk with heavenly holiness and intentional humility here on Earth.

Our Daily Oxygen

Let's be honest. Sometimes this journey with Jesus is draining and exhausting. But it's in fellowship and koinonia that relationships find the needed oxygen

---

[3] http://www.kingdomcitizens.org/citizenship-pt-3-the-concept-of-dual-citizenship.html.

to flourish and grow here on Earth. Amid all the heightened racial tension and polarization, renewed fellowship is desperately needed now more than ever.

Friends, we live in a time when many people are journeying alone, not realizing that isolation deprives them of life-giving oxygen. We have strayed so far from koinonia that we have been deprived of the necessary oxygen to thrive through these uncertain times. Could that be why the disciples chose to fish and do life together—to obtain the oxygen needed to live after the crucifixion of Jesus?

In Japan, oxygen bars sell oxygen for recreational use and also to combat pollution. Individuals choose flavored scents to enhance their experience, and some bars also use aromatic oils. Sadly, we have strayed so far from koinonia that we have forgotten that when followers of Jesus gather in fellowship, we're also gathering various flavors of people who add to our lives—and by God's grace, we don't even have to buy the oxygen because Jesus paid for it all!

I adopted a morning routine of koinonia almost three years ago. Every morning at 6:30 a.m., six other men and I meet to get the "oxygen" we need to face our daily challenges. This group is called Shift 180, and every man is a devoted husband, father, and friend. But our greatest commonality is our passion for God, our love of people, and our hunger for transformation. Being together in fellowship with these men every day is my equivalent of a double shot of espresso.

This daily oxygen and double shot of accountability and encouragement leave each of us feeling better physically and empowered spiritually to be the men we've been called to be. We hope to replicate this, reproducing Shift 180 gatherings around the nation where other men can acquire the oxygen they need to thrive in faith, family, and finances, and ultimately to make better disciples of Jesus Christ for the transformation of the world.

Research has proven through the 21/90 Rule that it takes twenty-one days to make a habit and ninety days to make it a permanent lifestyle change. At Shift 180, we have found that to be so true. Now it's almost second nature, a no-brainer, that at 6:30 a.m., we are going to be together. When I miss a gathering, it feels like something is missing. Not only is my day off-kilter, but I feel emotionally off-balance.

Through the journey over these last few years, we've discovered that being together daily cultivates oxygen and creates the spiritual alignment needed for us to love others as we love ourselves. As a group of men, we sharpen each other's saws and share creative, innovative ideas. But when I fail to connect in community with my brothers, I'm depleted and out of alignment. I start focusing on myself, and slowly, I begin to embrace the rugged individualism that negatively impacts my relationship with God and my commitment to family. So, every day, I seek to stay connected in community and fight never to do life alone.

I believe the global disruption brought by COVID-19 is forcing followers of Jesus to value fellowship and begin living as an Acts 2 community to experience transformative power. Unfortunately, we live in a society where individualism is so prevalent, and thus, there is an increase in substance abuse, mental health challenges, and suicide. Doing life alone has become the norm. In his book *Bowling Alone*, Robert Putnam says there are now fewer bowling leagues as more people choose to bowl alone.[4] But going from a "bowling alone" mentality to a "bowling league" mindset requires a drastic shift. It's much the same with the Christian community. From the inception of Jesus' new kingdom lifestyle, the disciples were never meant to fish—or bowl—alone. Instead, they lived life together in the context of modern-day bowling leagues or deep-sea fishing teams. Even when they were sent out on their mission to spread the Good News, Jesus always sent

---

[4] Robert D. Putnam, *Bowling Alone: The Collapse and Revival of American Community* (Simon & Schuster; Revised updated ed., October 13, 2020).

the disciples out two by two. Early in Jesus' earthly ministry, this was a reminder: one is never meant to journey alone.

When the disciples embarked on this challenging journey called The Way, they realized they needed oxygen from one another to survive. As Hebrews 10 points out, "And let us consider how we may spur one another on toward love and good deeds, not giving up meeting together, as some are in the habit of doing, but encouraging one another..." (Hebrews 10:24-25 NIV). The early church met daily to be encouraged and inspired and to keep moving forward despite unseen danger and highly possible persecution.

Grace and Power Found around the Table

The disciples also realized koinonia was deepened through sharing the sacred tradition of Holy Communion. It was a custom when they gathered to break bread and share a meal together. These meals modeled what it meant for the disciples to experience an intimate, shared life with Jesus. Amid constant persecution and attack, the people of the early church needed communion to remind them of the words of Jesus, who promised to always be with them. Scripture shares, "While they were eating, Jesus took bread, blessed it, broke it, and gave it to the disciples and said, 'Take and eat. This is my body.' He took a cup, gave thanks, and gave it to them, saying, 'Drink from this, all of you'" (Matthew 26:26-27 CEB).

Jesus knew fellowship would be developed around the table through the sacrament of Holy Communion. Holy Communion is both an act of thanksgiving and a reminder of the Passover meal, which was a celebration of God's liberating act of grace toward the Israelites in their deliverance from bondage to freedom. Through this sacred meal, we are reminded that regardless of the blatant injustice, oppression, and racism we encounter, we are forgiven of sin and delivered to new life through Jesus' sacrificial love. Jesus knew amazing things happen at the table.

Yet we currently live in a time when families have forgotten about the power and importance of sacred traditions at the table. According to the Centers for Disease Control, when families eat together at the table, it develops children's self-esteem, increases communication, and builds stronger family bonds.[5] Eating together as a family today is just as important as it was in the past.

When our kids were growing up, there was a rule in our home that no texting was allowed when we ate at

---

[5] https://www.cdc.gov/publichealthgateway/field-notes/2019/ky-dinner-table.html.

the table. If I caught them texting, they had to pass me their phone. Teens are so good with texting that they often can do it without looking. One time, our daughter Lauren was texting with her hands under the table. As she texted, she continued looking directly at me, but little did she know, I could see the phone's reflection in her glasses. You guessed it; she had to pass me her phone. It's so important we realize breaking bread at the table is a sacred tradition that should always be honored, whether at the relational family table or the Christian family table.

Not only was the time Jesus and the disciples spent together around the table sacred, but it was also a time of much-needed fellowship. They broke bread with glad and sincere hearts. Through fellowship, the early church discovered a sense of enjoyment with others in their community. As Scripture reminds us in Proverbs 17:22a (CEB), "A joyful heart helps healing."

As we continue to navigate this season of disruption, followers of Jesus must learn how to have fun together. Unfortunately, many believe being in a relationship with Jesus is boring, rigid, and routine. To surrender one's life to Jesus as Lord and Savior doesn't mean one must stop enjoying a good movie, a favorite concert, or even a good glass of wine. Remember, Jesus calls us to develop an authentic relationship with him. He does not ask us to follow a set of rigid religious rules.

After my brain surgery, I realized I must affirm this incredible gift of life daily. My personal mantra is to embrace life! To embrace life means to live in the present, to live intentionally with purpose, and to live every day with passion. So don't wait until you have a tragic event to embrace life every day. Remember, once you possess a right-side mindset, following Jesus can be fun, exciting, and adventuresome.

I'm convinced the sound of laughter is far more contagious than any cough, sniffle, or sneeze. When laughter is shared in community, it binds people together, increases joy, and cultivates authentic relationships. Laughter also strengthens your immune system, boosts your energy, decreases pain, and protects your heart and mind from stress. Best of all, like oxygen, laughter is priceless medicine, both fun and free! Author Anne Lamott once called laughter "carbonated holiness."

With so much unrest and uncertainty in today's church, I believe we need more "carbonated holiness." We must loosen up and not take life too seriously. A great message to declare to the "nones" and "dones" (those who don't participate in church and those who have left the church) is that having fun as a follower of Jesus is not only essential, it's biblical. I once heard a seasoned woman say some people are so serious about following Jesus and so heavenly-minded that they are no earthly good. If the disruption of the pandemic has taught us nothing else, it's taught us that we need to live our lives realizing, as hip-hop artist Drake prophetically says, YOLO—You Only Live Once. (That's for my hip-hopsters.)

In my formative years, following Jesus was a duty. But now that I'm seasoned and grayer, I follow him out of desire.

So often in life, we try to journey alone without realizing that this life of following Jesus was meant to be shared with others. I contend it's in fellowship with other followers of Jesus that the full essence of God is experienced. Consider David. Although David was the greatest king in Israel, he realized the importance and power of fellowship, as he wrote in Psalm 133:1 (NIV), "How good and pleasant it is when God's people live together in unity!"

God is pleased when believers live together in unity. When there's intentionality to live, work, and even worship together, it cultivates an atmosphere for unlimited possibilities. David could testify that when there's togetherness or unity, God blesses everything within the fellowship.

Right-side Gatherings

Highlighted by the pandemic's disruption, doing ministry on the left side has snuffed out the flame of innovation that ignites creativity and imagination in church leaders. This lack of innovation and imagination often hinders church leaders from going places others deem secular and unholy to cultivate new relationships. But Jesus reminds the disciples in Matthew 18:20 that where two or three are gathered, God is there. Jesus never saw things as either sacred or secular. Jesus was known for breaking bread with liars, tax collectors, and sinners. It was always his custom to hang out with the least, the last, the lost, and the left-outs. Jesus clearly demonstrates that anything God creates has redemptive value and purpose.

Leaders must shift their thinking and trust that everywhere followers of Jesus go, we must go too and change the atmosphere—even if it's an unpopular place or with forsaken people.

As we continue life with a right-side mindset, gathering spaces must go beyond the traditional church potluck, hymn-singing, and time of sharing joys and concerns. These activities aren't bad things, but the truth is people are desperately seeking something radical, something relevant, and something real. People are fed up with attending gatherings that are familiar, predictable, and comfortable. They yearn for gatherings where they can experience deeper meaning, authentic purpose, and true belonging, gatherings which usually happen in unexpected places with ordinary people who encounter an extraordinary God. In keeping with John 21:6, these are right-side gathering spaces.

What might a right-side gathering entail? In August 2021, God reignited my prophetic imagination to create a right-side gathering space called "Holy Smoke." The goal of Holy Smoke is to cultivate relevant conversation in a relaxed atmosphere that leads to real community and life transformation—all while smoking a good cigar at Top 10 Cigars, a local cigar lounge in Houston.

Believe it or not, cigars are a nearly $20 billion industry. Now, like my mother, you're probably wondering why it sounds like I am promoting tobacco use. My response is that it's not about smoking cigars per se, but rather about meeting people in a place where they can enjoy conversation—creating community—while savoring a cigar. Jesus used fishing to make new disciples, so why not use cigars to do the same? Remember, right-side gatherings: unexpected places with ordinary people where one can encounter an extraordinary God.

As I pondered Holy Smoke, I wondered: what if the local church became a right-side gathering? Fresh Expressions is the closest model of this. According to Path 1, a church-planting division of Discipleship Ministries, the Fresh Expressions movement is a form of church for our changing culture, established primarily for the benefit of those who are not yet part of any church. (To learn more, check out *Fresh Expressions: A New Kind of Methodist Church for People Not in Church* by United Methodist Bishop Ken Carter and Audrey Warren.)

With Fresh Expressions, people who stopped going to a local church can experience a different expression and encounter with God on any given day. Examples might include karaoke night at a pub or studying the Bible while enjoying a specially crafted beer. Dr. Barry Sloan, a Methodist pastor living in Germany where there has been a rapid increase in atheism, provides community and spiritual growth through whiskey tasting. INSPIRE ministries provides a Fresh Expression in a community where Jesus is now being made known through whiskey tasting. These kinds of faith communities may not happen in a traditional sanctuary or on Sunday.

Battlefield Farm & Gardens in Knoxville, Tennessee, also provides another example of a Fresh Expression. This faith community takes place in a garden where people who are burned out on traditional religion gather.

Pastor Chris Battle delivers a message, and instead of altar calls, the people tend to fifty raised gardens of kale, squash, eggplant, and tomatoes. They also clean chicken coops and manage compost piles. According to a featured segment on National Public Radio, when people attend, they are looking to connect with Jesus in a community of like-minded believers with a passion for gardening. Battlefield Farm offers a different kind of spiritual community. The people show up with their Bibles to learn, or they come and simply dig in the dirt.[6] When I reflect on this Fresh Expression, the words of Psalm 34:8, "Taste and see that the Lord is good," has a brand-new meaning.

Fresh Expressions offers right-side ministry models that can provide elements to cultivate community and curate experiences that are uncommon, uncertain, and uncomfortable.

During the pandemic, God renewed my perspective on fellowship and gave me creative insight into right-side gatherings. Because I'm no longer the pastor of a local church, I have unexpected opportunities. For the first time, I have witnessed people doing life together and experiencing koinonia at brunch, one of the new sacred spaces that happens on the weekends. I've discovered

---

[6] http://www.npr.org/2022/12/10/1141010320/as-attendance-dips-churches-change-to-stay-relevant-for-a-new-wave-of-worshipper.

brunch is a safe gathering space where you can break bread, share stories, and even have communion (mimosa and biscuits). Okay, I'm kidding—mostly. I believe that God may be calling someone reading this chapter right now to ignite their imagination and passion and develop a right-side gathering that consists of karaoke singing, cigar smoking, compost piling, and whiskey tasting.

Bottom line, we need more right-side gathering spaces where followers of Jesus can experience the unconditional love, the double shot of accountability and encouragement, and all the oxygen needed to experience renewed fellowship and koinonia.

And who knows? Maybe when we gather in these right-side spaces, we can experience the sort of Acts 2:47 church that causes Christianity to grow daily.

Questions for Reflection

1. Who holds you accountable? Where do you find your daily oxygen and get your double shot of encouragement and support? Do you have a group of friends who bring out the best in you?

2. How often does your family eat together at the table? What family tradition around the table do you remember growing up?

3. Are you following Jesus because of a legalistic duty or out of a loving desire for Jesus?

4. What ideas do you have for a right-side gathering in your community?

CHAPTER THREE
Reevaluating Leadership

By Mike Bowie

"The ultimate measure of a man is not where he stands in moments of comfort, but where he stands at times of challenge and controversy."

Dr. Martin Luther King, Jr.

As I reflect on this quote by Dr. King, I am immediately drawn to the leadership of Peter in John 21:3-4. As a disciple, Peter's true leadership and resilience were often revealed during tests and trials. Whenever he faced any challenges, he would either react or respond. Unfortunately, he was accustomed to reacting more than responding.

Emotions trigger both reactions and responses, and there's a difference between the two.

Reacting versus Responding

To *react* means personalizing an emotion and making an immediate choice or decision without thinking.

Reacting is usually rooted in the flesh and triggered by fear, anger, or surprise. Whenever we feel attacked, we often personalize the situation and react.

So, what causes this reaction? Within the autonomic nervous system of the brain is the amygdala. The amygdala is what triggers the fight, flight, or freeze reaction. Although Peter was one of the most beloved disciples of Jesus, he often operated out of the amygdala.

On one occasion, in John 18:10, when Jesus was about to be arrested, Peter sought to defend Jesus by cutting off the ear of Malchus, a high priest. Even though this erratic behavior was very impulsive, Peter felt his actions were justified. Peter often *reacted* versus *responded*. Remember, it's natural to have a physiological response when our emotions are triggered. I can relate. I have often reacted out of fear, only to experience negative consequences. In my years of following Jesus, I've discovered it's okay to possess fear, but we just can't let fear possess us. Now, I know that sounds preachy, but you must admit, it's great practical advice. How often have we reacted to a situation we couldn't control and later regretted the outcome? Maybe you didn't cut off an ear like Peter, but perhaps you said something derogatory when someone cut in line at the grocery store, or maybe it was going into a tirade after you discovered your french fries were cold. As leaders, we all face moments when our amygdala is triggered, and we must choose whether to react or respond.

Responding to a situation is quite different from reacting. When one responds to an unexpected situation, a person takes the time to think, process, and calculate an action. A response is made calmly, free from anxiety. The ability to respond calmly to a situation is rooted in the prefrontal cortex, the area of the brain that helps us control our thoughts and actions. The prefrontal cortex helps the amygdala see stressful events as a little less scary or frustrating. The main job of the prefrontal cortex is to control our emotional responses to fear and stress so that we do not get too stressed out.

Unlike Peter, Jesus seldomly *reacted*; rather, he *responded* to some of the most challenging situations. In Luke 23:34, as Jesus was being crucified, he responded to his enemies by forgiving them. That's right—as Jesus was being crucified, he was giving a master class on leadership.

When a leader is facing the greatest challenge of their life, they must choose to respond to the situation in a composed manner versus reacting to the situation in an anxious, impulsive manner. Let's be honest. We have faced challenges many times and reacted like Peter instead of responding like Jesus.

One of the greatest traits of a good leader is the ability to forgive those who intentionally hurt you. Remember, forgiveness isn't for the person who hurt you; forgiveness is for you. Forgiveness is a gift we give ourselves for those who have trespassed against us. When I think about forgiveness, I am reminded of the late Nelson Mandela, South Africa's first Black president. He once said, "Resentment is like drinking poison and then hoping it will kill your enemies." At the end of the day, when we refuse to forgive someone, we only hurt ourselves.

As a result of Mandela's resistance against apartheid, he was sentenced to life in prison and spent twenty-seven years in the Robben Island prison. Upon his early release, Mandela decided he could not harbor hate in his heart for his accusers. He knew it was easy to hate and harder to forgive. Mandela said, "Forgiveness liberates the soul. It removes fear. That is why it is such a powerful weapon."

Throughout Peter's ministry, he was very judgmental and often withheld forgiveness of others. In Matthew 18:21-22, Peter asks Jesus how many times he should forgive his brother who sinned against him. Jesus responds by saying, "Seven times seventy." In other words, there's no limit to the number of times we should offer forgiveness to those who have sinned against us.

We might think it's impossible, but just as God freely forgives us daily for our sins, we should forgive others the same way.

If you react to situations like Peter and respond to situations like Jesus, you're in good company. Very seldom does God base our ability to lead on the number of times we've reacted impulsively, but instead, on the times we have intentionally responded to God's grace and mercy. Despite Peter's character flaws of being anxious, impatient, and impulsive, God still used him to start the first church. This example is an awesome reminder that God never calls those who are equipped but always equips those whom God calls! You may have some character flaws, but they have nothing to do with the unmerited favor God has to enhance your leadership.

Being Aware of Your Emotional Intelligence

During this season of disruption, I believe God wants to expand our leadership capacity, but we, too, must learn how to respond to tests and trials rather than reacting. One of the best ways to accomplish this is through understanding emotional intelligence.

Emotional intelligence is your ability to recognize and understand emotions in yourself and others and your ability to use this awareness to manage your behavior and relationships. This has nothing to do with your intelligence quotient, your IQ, but has everything to do with understanding yourself emotionally—your emotional quotient, or EQ. When you possess a healthy EQ, you do not allow your emotions to cloud your thinking and clutter your judgment. Far too often, we can't control our initial emotions or feelings, but what we can control are the thoughts that follow the emotions. When you have a high EQ, you have the power to decide how you will respond to emotions. (I highly recommend the book *Emotional Intelligence 2.0* by Travis Bradberry and Jean Greaves to help you understand this better.)

Many times, we allow traumatic life events to hijack our emotions, triggering certain reactions we often live to regret. Jesus was always trying to increase the disciples' EQs. On one occasion in the Gospel of Mark, Jesus and the disciples are crossing the Sea of Galilee and get caught in a traumatic storm. Because of a low EQ, the disciples allow the storm to trigger their fear and dictate their faith. When the storms of life consume our attention, it's difficult to see Christ working in our lives. There have been times in our lives when we've allowed the storms in our relationships, careers, and finances to hinder Jesus from working in our lives. But when we possess a healthy EQ, we discover that fear constantly looks at the storm while faith constantly looks at the Savior who calms the storms.

For those who may currently be in a storm, remember, through the power of the Holy Spirit, we can recognize emotional triggers and manage those emotions well, ultimately leading to positive results—as opposed to regrets—in our lives. When we have a healthy EQ, we realize that regardless of how frightening a storm may be, God has the power to balance our emotions and calm any storm.

Even after Peter's initial call to follow Jesus, he often reacted to situations when he should have responded to them. Impatient and impulsive, Peter frequently spoke without thinking. However, despite all of Peter's character flaws, Jesus allowed him to be a person of influence. Author and business consultant Kenneth H. Blanchard states, "The key to successful leadership is influence, not authority." Jesus elevated Peter as the leader of the disciples, and he was one of three in Jesus' inner circle. But Peter's influence wasn't derived from his personal authority; rather, it came from his personal relationship with Jesus. Peter customarily set the tone for the other disciples to follow. On one occasion, when society began questioning Jesus' divinity, Jesus approached Peter and asked him, "Who do you say that I am?" Peter says, "You are Christ, the Son of God." Jesus says that flesh and blood did not reveal this, and he goes on to tell Peter that on this rock or confession, he would build his church. It is encouraging to know that even when we react and make mistakes, God can still use us to start a transformative movement.

Discovering and Maximizing Your Strengths

After the horrid reality of Jesus' crucifixion and the trauma that followed, Peter decided to do what he did well: go fishing. Before Jesus called him as a disciple, Peter had been a professional fisherman, and now that Jesus was no longer around, he felt comfortable returning to what came naturally. Whether Peter realized it or not, this is one of the greatest traits of leadership: operating in your strength.

About eighteen years ago, my leadership was enhanced when I discovered the power of knowing your strengths as the teaching pastor at Ginghamsburg Church. The Rev. Sue Nelson Kibbey, who at that time was the executive pastor at Ginghamsburg Church, was a huge promoter of StrengthsFinder™, an assessment that measures your innate abilities based on how you usually think, behave, and feel. Dr. Don Clifton, founder and father of strengths-based psychology who began the movement and co-authored *Now, Discover your Strengths*, concluded that humans possess thirty-four common strengths. Clifton defines "strengths" as "the ability to consistently provide near-perfect performance." Talent plus investment equals strength, Clifton theorized. Talent is our natural way of thinking, feeling, and behaving, while investment is the time spent practicing our skills development and building our knowledge base.[7]

Once we discover our strengths, we feel fully alive, are motivated to go to work, and are excited and eager to serve others. Unfortunately, we've become obsessed with focusing on our weaknesses, not our strengths. Far too often, we acknowledge our deficits and shortcomings, ultimately becoming "professional weakness experts." We give too much time, energy, and attention to what we don't do well, which ultimately hinders us from living with purpose, productivity, and passion.

Growing up, we were told we must be well-rounded individuals, and perhaps we taught the same to our children. My child could get an A in English, an A in science, a B in history, and a C in math, and unfortunately, I'd focus most of my attention on what? The C in math. Now, I'm not saying Cs aren't okay, but at the end of the day, we must maximize our children's strengths and stop focusing on their

---

[7] Marcus Buckingham and Donald O. Clifton, *Now, Discover Your Strengths* (Free Press, 2001).

weaknesses. Maybe my child was not meant to become a mathematician. So why did I focus so much on that C?

It's impossible to be perfectly well-rounded. Even the great Michael Jordan realized his strength was basketball, not baseball. Although he gave some time and attention to baseball, he realized it was a far better choice to maximize his strengths in basketball and not fixate on his baseball weaknesses. I'm not a huge Jordan fan, but I daresay he is legendary if not one of the greatest NBA players.

Bottom line: we are not called to be well-rounded. Instead, we are called to maximize our strengths and, most of all, stay in our own lane. As the late hip-hop artist and social entrepreneur Nipsey Hussle once said, "Stay in your own lane because there's no traffic." That's what Peter did that day when he went fishing. But on this particular day, the fish weren't biting. Even though Peter was operating in the correct profession, he was in the wrong position. And because of his influence, all the disciples followed him and operated in their profession the same way—on the left side.

If you recall from the previous chapter, the left side—again, not a political term but an alternative position of unlimited possibilities—is where things are certain, common, and comfortable. I believe the disciples were so certain they would catch some fish that they got comfortable. After all, they assumed if they caught fish on the left side before, they would surely catch some fish again. Isn't it amazing how we can get so comfortable living our routines and just assume everything will always work out? Unfortunately, we can't be so certain. I cannot assume I know the outcome just because I've been doing this for years and invested in my talent for so long. That's one thing the pandemic's disruption taught me: there's a danger of getting so accustomed to doing things *my* way with *my* talents that I overlook my need for God. Servanthood leadership is cultivated when we depend on and connect to Jesus Christ.

Could it be the disciples were so confident in their talents that they didn't see the need for Jesus? Could it be that way for us today? Now, you're probably saying that sounds like a contradiction. After all, I said earlier that we could maximize life when we discover our strengths. But we cannot forget that we are called to co-partner with God to expand and further the kingdom—and this goes far beyond maximizing individual strengths. So, here's a new, right-side kingdom equation: God's power + my strengths = supernatural possibilities. Once we fully surrender to the Lordship of Jesus and fully embrace our unique strengths, amazing things can happen.

That's how it was in the Acts 2 community.

For decades here in America, we have been doing life using our own left-side strengths with so much certainty, all without fully including Jesus. And like the disciples, we have "caught" nothing but injustice, poverty, and all the "isms." History has proven that whenever God is excluded from our daily affairs, we will have White privilege, gun violence, and a growing wealth gap. When God is slowly removed from facets of our lives, we can expect negative consequences. As John Wesley said, "What one generation tolerates, the next generation will embrace."

To paraphrase the words of both Nipsey Hussle and John Wesley, I believe it's time to reassess the leadership needed to change the trajectory in America. We currently live on the left side in a capitalistic, materialistic, and individualistic society. Yet, Jesus is there, yelling from the shore, saying, "Cast your nets on the right side for an amazing catch of new multigenerational leaders! I dare you to shift."

New Right-side Multigenerational Leaders

It's time for a new right-side group of multigenerational leaders to rise and co-partner with God to be the change the world is waiting for.

In Psalm 145:4, King David declares, "Generation after generation stands in awe of your work; each one tells stories of your mighty acts" (MSG). Here, David is simply saying that every generation has a responsibility to tell its own story about God's mighty acts. When one generation fails to tell its story, the following generation suffers.

I believe we are eroding Christian values because we are no longer telling the stories of God's mighty acts. When the redeemed aren't saying anything, we're allowing the values of the culture to dictate the values of the kingdom!

For the first time in the history of America, there are five generations influencing culture, the workforce, and society simultaneously. Because of this reality and the significant differences between each generation, I contend that to have effective, right-side, multigenerational leaders, our churches, organizations, and corporations must clearly understand the traits of each generation. George Barna, founder of the Barna Group, specializes in researching religious trends and behaviors. According to Barna, we must understand and respect each generation to lead an effective multigenerational ministry or organization. Let's take a look at each generation:

Traditionalist or "Silent" Generation (born 1925-1945)

The LP, the long-playing 33 1/3-rpm record, was introduced during this generation. There are approximately eighteen to twenty million of this generation in the world today.

They are called the Silent Generation because they worked hard and kept quiet during times of war and economic challenges. This generation believes children should be seen and not heard. Because of the Great Depression and World War II, the birth rate during this period was extremely low. A generalized description of this generation is as follows:

- **Core values:** Loyalty, patriotism, patience, saving money, trust in government
- **Attributes: Committed** to company, conservative, dedicated, does more with less, strong work ethic.
- **View of work/life balance:** Work hard to maintain job security; keep work and personal life separate.
- **Keys to working with this group:** Understand that they think work is not supposed to be fun. While they follow rules well, they do want to know procedures.
- **Retirement plan:** Put in thirty years, retire, and live off pension/savings.
- **Family experience:** Raised in a traditional nuclear family (man, woman, children).

Traditionalists consider work a privilege, and they're considered the wealthiest generation. Traditionalists believe that to get ahead in their careers, they had to earn their own way through hard work. They don't trust overnight success and aren't risk-takers. Also, for this generation, authority is based on seniority and tenure.

Most of this generation possess Christian values and believe Christianity is very important to one's faith. They support the church with their time, talents, and treasures. Many of the Silent Generation were raised in the church, and it was a given that their children would grow up in the church as well. This generation needs to tell their story about how they had to trust God with limited finances during the Great Depression and WWII era. This generation has a responsibility to mentor and model to the next generation how to save money but still live with an abundant/not scarcity mindset.

Traditionalists have generally lived their lives with a left-side mindset.[8]

Baby Boomers (born 1946-1964)

This generation saw a shift from the 33 1/3-rpm to the 45-rpm record, and in 1964, the 8-track tape was

---

[8] https://www.usf.edu/hr-training/documents/lunch-bytes/generationaldifferenceschart.pdf.

introduced. They are called Baby Boomers because of the "boom," or significant number of births during that post-WWII era. Today there are about seventy-two million Baby Boomers, and nearly 70 million are expected to retire over the next decade. Forty percent of Boomers have smartphones and use technology. Many in this generation have at least one social media platform, usually Facebook. This generation views work as a career rather than a job. The majority prefer face-to-face communication over texting. A generalized description of this generation is as follows:

- **Core values:** Antiwar, antigovernment, equal rights, equal opportunities, personal gratification, spend now/worry later.
- **Attributes:** Ability to handle a crisis, ambitious, challengers of authority, competent, competitive, live to work.
- **View of work/life balance:** Hesitant about taking too much time off work for fear of losing their place in the corporate team.
- **Keys to working with this group:** They expect their work and themselves to matter. They do well in teams.
- **Retirement plan:** If I retire, who am I? I haven't saved any money, so I need to work, at least part-time.
- **Family experience:** Raised in a "Ward and June Cleaver" family where the mom stayed home.

This generation also believes in the importance of religion, but they are anti-establishment. Unlike the previous generation, the Boomers are committed to career advancement and moving up the "corporate ladder." Boomers also have one of the highest divorce rates of any other generation.

Boomers need to share their stories about how God gave them strength through challenging and trying times, such as Vietnam, the civil rights movement, and even Woodstock. This generation intentionally mentors and reminds other generations that while education and career advancement are important, life is about more than just making money; life is about making meaning.

Boomers tend to live with a left-side mindset but with some right-side tendencies. [9]

Generation X (born 1965-1979)

This generation embraced the compact cassette tape and the Sony Walkman, introduced in 1979.

There are currently forty-four to fifty million Americans in this generation. Often called the "sandwich" or "forgotten" generation, they are often overlooked between Boomers and Millennials. Unlike

---

[9] https://www.usf.edu/hr-training/documents/lunch-bytes/generationaldifferenceschart.pdf.

the Boomers, Generation X places a premium on family time and has a different attitude about work. A generalized description of this generation is as follows:

- **Core Values:** Balance, diversity, entrepreneurial spirit, fun, highly educated, independent, lack organizational loyalty.

- **Attributes:** Adaptable, flexible, results-driven, self-sufficient, skeptical of institutions, work to live.

- **View of work/life balance:** Because their parents are Boomer workaholics, they focus on a clearer balance between work and family.

- **Keys to working with this group:** They want independence in the workplace and time to pursue other interests. They want to have fun at work, and they want to use the latest technology.

- **Retirement plan:** I've saved my money, so I may retire early. I may want different experiences, and I may change careers.

- **Family experience:** Raised as latch-key kids. Women are expected to work outside the home. This is the first daycare/dual-income family generation.

Generation X is so committed to family that a major shift occurred. After the Blue Laws were officially abolished in 1985, shopping, going to the movies, buying alcohol, and sports activities began to compete with Christianity and the importance of the church.

Generation X live their lives with a left-side mindset, but they are open to a right-side perspective.[10]

Millennials/Generation Y (born 1980-1995)

This generation's experience includes the CD, the MP3, and the iPod, and they tend to see the world differently from other generations. With numbers estimated as high as seventy-three million Americans, Millennials have an entrepreneurial spirit. The generalized characteristics of this generation are as follows:

- **Core values:** Achievement, avid consumerism, education, civic duty, diversity, social life, globalism.

- **Attributes:** Ambitious but not entirely focused, most educated generation, extremely technology savvy. They are diversity-focused, multicultural, innovative—think outside the proverbial box, individualistic yet group-oriented, open to new ideas, self-absorbed with a strong sense of entitlement, and very patriotic (shaped by 9/11).

- **View of work/life balance:** Not only do they balance work with life, but they also balance community involvement and self-development.

- **Keys to working with this group:** They like a team-oriented workplace and want to work

---

[10] https://www.usf.edu/hr-training/documents/lunch-bytes/generationaldifferenceschart.pdf.

with bright, creative people. They provide variety and want to work with their friends.

- **Retirement plan:** The jury is still out, but they will probably be like Gen Xers, perhaps also saving money to retire early or change careers.
- **Family experience:** Merged, modern families. They are coddled kids with trophies for eighth place.

Millennials are the first generation of digital natives. They crave meaningful work that contributes to their organization's mission, but they are also prone to frequent job changes as they seek employment on their own terms. They seek supervisors and mentors who are highly engaged in their professional development. For example, almost eighty percent of Millennials report they'd like their manager/boss to act like a coach or mentor.

This generation is skeptical about politics and the institutional church. They have seen church scandals with the fall of prominent religious leaders (e.g., Jim Bakker and Jimmy Swaggart) and political scandals like the President Bill Clinton/Monica Lewinsky affair. Because of their skepticism about the institutional church and spiritual leaders, they are compelled to give to causes outside the church. Many Millennials are now running for political office because of the immoral leadership of elected officials. Since the pandemic, there has been a shift in the political system, and more

Millennials were elected to Congress in 2020 than in any other year.

Millennials live their lives with left-side tendencies, but the majority possess a right-side mindset.[11]

Generation Z (born 1996-2010)

This generation enjoys cloud-based music from Google, Spotify, and Apple Music, among the most popular. Encompassing ninety-one million people, this generation makes up 25.9 percent—the largest portion—of the United States population and contributes about $44 billion to the American economy. While new to the workforce, their entrepreneurial spirit is strong. More than seventy percent want to start their own businesses, and three percent already have. A post-9/11 generation, they are all too familiar with terrorism and Transportation Security Administration screening in airports.

This is the first generation where atheism is accepted as the norm. The general characteristics of this generation are as follows:

- **Core values:** Quick results, multitasking, very frugal, independent, entrepreneurial, and global thinking.

---

[11] https://www.usf.edu/hr-training/documents/lunch-bytes/generationaldifferenceschart.pdf.

- **Attributes:** Less focused, addicted to technology, diversity-focused and multicultural, a strong sense of entitlement, liberal views on politics and sexuality.
- **View of work/life balance:** This generation prefers to work in technological spaces with the latest gadgets. Working remotely is valued and expected. They need changing and challenging projects to combat boredom.
- **Keys to working with this group:** They want to work with bright, creative people. They provide variety and want to work with friends and be the boss.
- **Retirement plan:** The jury is still out, just like the Millennials.
- **Family experience:** This generation is more accepting of same-sex marriages.[12]

This is the first generation that only knows a right-side mindset.

As my denomination, The United Methodist Church, continues to splinter and discern its way forward, I contend that ample time, energy, and financial resources must be invested into Generation Z. Investing in their leadership may not seem like a good return on investment now, but this will be the main generation making crucial decisions in 2050 when society

---

[12] https://www.usf.edu/hr-training/documents/lunch-bytes/generationaldifferenceschart.pdf.

drastically shifts from majority Anglo/White to majority Latino/Brown people.

Remember Psalm 145:4, "Generation after generation stands in awe of your work; each one tells stories of your mighty acts" (MSG). Now that we have been equipped and empowered with this multigenerational information, we must do all we can to help Generation Z understand why Christ matters. Although this generation has a different perspective on life, it's time for us to cultivate new right-side leaders to rise up and co-partner with God to be the change our churches, communities, and world is waiting for. I dare you to shift!

Questions for Reflection

1. Do you normally react or respond when you are in a challenging situation?

2. What are your strengths and talents? Do you utilize those strengths and talents to better your relationships and further the kingdom, or do you focus more on your weaknesses?

3. Have there been storms in your life when you have allowed fear to hinder Jesus? Has there ever been a time when your emotions allowed fear to dictate your faith?

4. What generation do you fall into? Do you identify with the generalized characteristics described for your generation?

5. What insight did you gain from reading the general characteristics given for the other generations?

CHAPTER FOUR

Rethinking Entrepreneurship

By Stephen Handy

The best way to predict the future is to create it.
Peter Drucker

Questions can stimulate the mind! Rev. Dr. Lovett H. Weems, Jr., is distinguished professor of church leadership and senior consultant of the Lewis Center for Church Leadership at Wesley Theological Seminary in Washington, D.C. and former President of Saint Paul School of Theology, said, "Great leaders don't have great answers, but great leaders ask great questions." Most entrepreneurs and people of influence set out to solve problems. The key to solving problems is never to come up with a solution that doesn't understand the culture and the context. Entrepreneurs dive deep into understanding the problem and then emerge with at least one solution. After the Resurrection, Jesus engages the disciples to help them rethink their behaviors, patterns, and perceptions and instill hope so they can think more entrepreneurially.

Jesus, the originator of great questions, asserts himself and poses a question to the disciples about the operations of their family business: "Children, you have no fish, have you?" Jesus wants to know, "Is your business producing any results?" Not only were Jesus' followers becoming disciples, many, as fishermen, were already entrepreneurs. Fishing was the primary occupation of these disciples; it was their means of earning a living. After Jesus' death, his disciples quickly retreated to their old ways. In another way, Jesus is asking, "How's that working for you?" All segments of the church, non and for-profit, governmental must often ask the same question.

Have you ever retreated, gone back to the familiar because fear was driving you back to that place? Fear speaks loudly in order to lead us down the path of deception and division. Voices of deception and division happen daily in our minds and attempt to derail us from our mission. Every church, business, nonprofit, and governmental agency leader has missional objectives that keep the organization focused and faithful. Challenges become plentiful when we allow too many competing voices and conflicting strategies to prevent us from engaging in the mission. We end up joining the club of "missional drift," which happens to individuals and organizations.

Missional drift happens when we replace, or substitute, the mission of the church, entity, nonprofit, or organization for what *we* believe is more important. For example, several years ago, the leaders of McKendree United Methodist Church were holding a leadership session to determine our mission. As we were engaging in deep prayer, the spirit reminded us about Jesus' mission for the church as found in Luke:

> *The Spirit of the Lord is on me, because he has anointed me to proclaim good news to the poor. He has sent me to proclaim freedom for the prisoners and recovery of sight for the blind, to set the oppressed free, to proclaim the year of the Lord's favor.*
>
> **Luke 4:18-19 (NIV)**

In that moment, we realized our mission had already been given to us, and there was no way to improve upon it.

Spend More Time Asking Questions

The question remains, though: with so many voices, how do you determine which voice should prevail? We learn most by asking questions, not by having the answers. Early in school, I was taught not to ask questions, "just listen and do what I say." Nike has a great brand and motto, "Just Do It!" Often, my curiosity led me to ask, Just do what? Do it all? Do it right now? Do it alone or with a trusted friend and colleague? If I understand what I'm expected to do, there is a better chance that I might consider doing it, especially with someone else. Presenting questions can be pathways to transforming minds and hearts so that courageous and devoted leaders create spaces for innovative imagination.

Entrepreneurs, by definition, are compulsive risk-takers, constantly rethinking and leaning into life as a way forward. Not consumed by the past, entrepreneurs see beyond the obvious to opportunities for others. These opportunities are invitations to disrupt certain ways of being and thinking so that we can live into a life of anticipated abundance. As the disciples are anticipating a catch, their level of anticipation is extremely low.

Depression and trauma have disrupted their lives, causing deep mental health problems and crippling their physical bodies. Jesus their Savior is gone. "Trauma is not what happens to you but what happens inside you" is how I formulate it. Think of a car accident as what happened; the injury is what lasts.[13] Today, these same traumatic and emotional mental-health realities exist and can cause many leaders to become static in their ability to shift behavior.

Could it be that Jesus is asking, "Are you prepared

---

[13] Gabor Maté with Daniel Maté, *The Myth of Normal: Trauma, Illness & Healing in a Toxic Culture* (Avery, September 13, 2022).

for and anticipating a catch of abundance, or is it just an assignment?" In this case, it was about catching fish because these disciples were fishermen; their physical and mental health depended on the reality of abundance. No fisherman ever desires to return home fishless! No one works a full- or part-time job for no pay. Everyone expects a return on their investment. Jesus has invested in these disciples in hopes of seeing a fruitful return—not just fish but people. Jesus calls people into alignment, but we spend a disproportionate amount of time doing assignments that don't lead to alignment with God and others.

Learn to Listen to Understand Before Responding

In today's cultural context, leaders must create a culture of intentional and active listeners. Placing ourselves in the formation of culture, leaders have an obligation to be mindful and think critically before rendering an answer, listening with courage and humility. Leaders are often taught to be first, loud, and to always win. In his song, All I do is win, DJ Khaled sings a refrain, "All I do is win, win, no matter what."

In essence, one leadership characteristic that most leaders lack is empathetic listening, listening with the heart. Jesus has been listening with his heart and now proposes a question to the disciples: "Friends, haven't you caught any fish?" Maybe another way to pose this question in leadership roles is to be inquirers who explore the organization's "why." After some time in your profession, it's difficult when you have caught or secured nothing to show for your efforts. As Americans, we are driven to exhaustion trying to produce the next level of production quo, whatever entity we lead.

What are we willing to hear with our hearts and then with our ears? Listening is an undervalued gift of God. All leaders must learn to listen better. Often, we are rewarded for talking or speaking but very seldom for listening. As a child, I was *told* to listen but never *taught* to listen. Conversation is often our first mode of authentic, active listening. Active listening happens when we surpass our need to answer when the conversation is not over yet. But guess what? Very seldom do people take listening classes because people are rewarded for speaking. Shifting to become leaders who listen will take time and courage. Relationships should be measured by our ability to listen to others as opposed to speaking over each other.

Beyond being a reluctant leader in building the ark, Noah listens to God in order to save a remnant of humanity. Whether you believe the story or not, it's a tremendous example of what courageous listening and following instructions can do for you and your community. Noah is a family man and a hard worker when God disrupts his normal day to suggest a shift in his work effort, a way to think and act differently. God has said, Let's use your skill to build an ark. Can you hear Noah: What? Do you realize it hasn't rained yet? Noah could have easily said no to what he was hearing, the voice and instructions of God! Instead, Noah recognized that something in his community and society needed to change, and maybe this was a means to a better way. With critics within and beyond his family, Noah builds God's ark after hearing every little detail. He's an entrepreneur who understands and embraces risk.

When we hear a word, situation, or illustration in conversation, how many times do we get triggered and go on the defensive, hearing nothing else from that moment on? Leaders must understand that the human anatomy is formed with two ears and one mouth, not vice versa. So why do we spend twice as much time talking when we are designed to listen twice as much as we talk?

During their unproductive day, the disciples must answer Jesus with the truth: We have caught nothing, not one fish. Honesty is not only a great policy, but it also pushes us to an openness for something else. "No" is also a complete sentence. Notice what Jesus doesn't do. Jesus doesn't condemn them for being unproductive, wasting time, not focusing, being in the wrong place, or not praying about it. Jesus invites them to **"Cast the net to the right side of the boat"** and then says, **"You will find some."** Part of the challenge of shifting is the logistics of having all the supportive documentation and us building a thorough case to prove to others why we need to shift. Paralysis can get in the way of shifting our mindset, trusting, and having enough faith to move.

Courageous and resilient leaders have the humility to employ and place people around them who can offer different perspectives, especially when it differs from the status-quo mindset. It is common thought that creativity and innovation is positioned in the brain's right hemisphere, known as "right-brain thinkers," while "left-brain thinkers" are often thought to be analytical and logical. As discussed in earlier chapters, let's refer to static thinking as "left-side thinking"— and remember, "left-side" and "right-side" are not political terms in this conversation. Sometimes left-side thinking aligns with the past and simply tries to work harder and longer until there are different results, this mindset can diminish possibilities and momentum that brings progressive shifts. Left-side thinking leads to tremendous amounts of leadership and organizational burnout, and it can lack creativity and innovation when competency and uncertainty takes root in the culture.

Beware of Missional Drift

Several successful companies have modeled creativity and innovation until missional drift became the order of the day. For example, Blockbuster, a video rental company, refused to adapt or shift into a right-side mindset. First, Blockbuster lost out to a rental company called Redbox. While Blockbuster built huge warehouses to display videotapes for rental, Redbox shifted their strategy to focus on the convenience of localizing and placing their video rental machines where people frequently visited, like Walgreens, grocery stores, and gasoline stations. Soon, Blockbuster ended up closing their brick-and-mortar locations, and they started adding kiosk machines. But it was too late. Redbox had mastered the market concept. However, Redbox then settled and became a culture of left-side thinkers, and on-demand streaming shifted the thinking of consumers to shop online without leaving their homes. Netflix now rules the day, but beware, something different is inevitably on the horizon.

Mindset Shift Before Skill Set Focus

Organizational leaders with a right-side or other-side mindset listen with greater sensitivity and are connected to the spiritual realm. Right-side or other-side thinking represents a cultural shift wherein the leader is willing to experiment because they recognize they don't know enough and are willing to lean into people who know more. This mindset takes humility and is necessary for the entrepreneurial spirit to connect the dots to an alternative way of thinking. Levering our entrepreneurial spirit comes with prudent risks and potential growth and rewards.

Being willing to cast the net to the right side takes courage and risk because it involves shifting your mindset and physical posture to see, think, and act differently. The COVID pandemic forced the world to shut down left-side thinking because people were confined to their homes for school and work and limited in their faith formation. Everything closed except gasoline stations, hospitals, and grocery stores. Everyone was trying to figure out the right side of the boat—the organization, church, synagogue, mosque, corporation, and school. Buildings were vacant, with massive amounts of unused space. Some corporations and congregations (even before the pandemic) found themselves in the same predicament: tons of employees and parishioners and no building but still work that needed to be done. We are in a pandemic of paralysis! What do we do when we are paralyzed or stuck in neutral?

Innovation Can Emerge Within Us!

Leaders that emerge from a crisis are worth listening to and following. Why? There is something notable about leaders who are wired to emerge from the ashes of death and destructive thinking. I believe we all have the gene of entrepreneurship; it's buried underneath all the years of fear, death, anxiety, embarrassment, grief, doubt, shame, domestic violence, abuse, and neglect. You get the picture. Jesus endured all that destructive thinking so that we could rethink our way forward. Rev. Martin Luther King, Jr.'s "fierce urgency of now" suggests that for many of society's disinherited, Christian innovation is necessary, not optional. The status quo must be disrupted so that our communities can see and experience an alternative way because, at some time, humanity must realize we are interconnected and, therefore, interrelated.

Jesus' words penetrate our hearts and release the endorphins of our brains to help us recover our entrepreneurial spirit so that we can listen to the voice of abundance, the voice of connection, and, ultimately, the voice of Jesus Christ. One of the beautiful realities of Jesus' words is that they didn't stop when he died. As Jesus was resurrected, his words became transformative and allowed his disciples and others to experience an invitation to an alternative way of being. Jesus returned to offer everyone the gift of the Holy Spirit, to reconnect our minds and missionally shift our thinking on how to catch fish and how to relate to people. Same mission, but now we needed an alternative way. Listen, just shift to the other side. It's not easy because culture is built on repetition, which builds reputation. But, entities, organizations, governments, nonprofits, and faith communities must constantly examine themselves and seek to maximize their collective genius in order to connect with the least of these in our communities.

People must evolve by casting the net to the other side, "the right side." Leaders must be careful not to stagnate and become the ineffective side of productivity, creativity, and innovation.

After two decades of pastoral leadership at Dellrose United Methodist in Wichita, Kansas, Rev. Dr. Kevass Harding decided it was time to leverage his creative, innovative side of ministry and connect to the missional needs in his immediate community. As in most urban centers, affordable housing didn't exist. After wrestling with Scripture, the words of Jeremiah 29:11 (NIV)—"For I know the plans I have for you," declares the Lord, "plans to prosper you and not harm you, plans to give you HOPE and a future"—were impregnated with a vision and plan of action. In August 2017, Pastor Harding gave birth to HOPE Community Development Corporation—an acronym for Helping Other People Excel. As a result of deep levels of listening, prudent partnerships, and intentional collaboration with metro government, nonprofits, and the business community, HOPE's first affordable home will be completed in April 2023.

Mutual Respect and Responsibility

Leaders at all levels of the enterprise must create a culture of mutual responsibility and respectability. When people trust one another, anything can be talked about, and there is a greater probability of shifting behavior. Understand, though, that shifting takes time unless the situation is desperate and dire. That's where we find the disciples then and the nonprofits, government, and faith communities now in society. We are in desperate times, but we have options and alternatives. Effective leaders offer right-side thinking when they are positioned to see beyond the obvious—not perfectly but prophetically—so that people will be open to shifting and taking the next faithful step.

There's a story about a young boy whose mother

noticed the barn light was left on. She asked her son to take the flashlight and go turn the barn light off. After stepping outside, he realized how far the barn was in the dark, so he returned to the house. His mother walked outside with him toward the barn with the flashlight. She demonstrated that he needed to walk one step at a time toward the end of the shining light, and if he followed the end of the light, he would reach the barn in the dark. He walked towards the barn, taking one faithful step after another until he reached the barn and turned off the light.

Shifting from the loss of a loved one is never easy, but it becomes necessary over time. Although we may never move beyond the loss, we must move forward. Prior to Jesus appearing, the disciples returned to their comfortable ways, even after he had introduced them to patterns for abundant living. What keeps you from being curious enough to try another way? The disciples and others were suffering from broken hearts as they thought about the loss of their Savior. But then Jesus appears, and now their hearts and lives are awakened to rethink fishing again. In this moment, maybe they remembered their first encounter with Jesus:

> *As Jesus was walking beside the Sea of Galilee, he saw two brothers, Simon called Peter and his brother*

Andrew. They were casting a net into the lake, for they were fishermen. "Come, follow me," Jesus said, "and I will send you out to fish for people." At once they left their nets and followed him.

Mark 1:18-20 (NIV)

Leaders must cast vision and expect it to be accompanied by provision. Godly vision creates an alternative to the current reality. Neither vision nor the provision ever originated with the disciples. The GOD'S WORD Translation of James 1:17 states:

> *Every good present and every perfect gift comes from above, from the Father who made the sun, moon, and stars. The Father doesn't change like the shifting shadows produced by the sun and the moon.*

Expectation Comes with Courage

Expectancy comes when faith and hope connect. Everyone should have a daily expectation. Anyone in leadership needs to be expectant, bold, and courageous enough to stand in the gap and say, "Think about this differently!" Jesus is always that person who creates the environment to shift, but he also invites us to be the instigator for others to engage in an entrepreneurial exchange by asking them to shift their mindset.

Casting well means catching well! Sounds easy—

until we get stuck in our own way of doing life. Paul the Apostle writes to the church in Ephesus, which was also experiencing stagnant living from the left side. There's more to life than we know. Paul writes:

> *Now to him who by the power at work within us is able to accomplish abundantly far more than all we can ask or imagine, to him be glory in the church and in Christ Jesus to all generations, forever and ever. Amen.*
>
> **Ephesians 3:20-21 (NRSV)**

To accomplish more abundantly than we can ask or imagine, there must be alignment with God's order. **Beware, we must clear the distractions and negativity because they breed fear and frustration.**

After the disciples turn, think, and act differently, the net shifts to the other side, and guess what they discover? Yes! Abundance! The catch was enough—more than enough for themselves and others. The haul of fish could not even be secured by one boat. The multitude of people Jesus desires to align with is an expression of abundance. This abundance needs the community; it needs a collaborative effort. Thinking out of abundance—rather than fear of scarcity—is a mind shift, a resetting of mindset. If God had a nickname, it would be More Than Enough.

Recently, I listened to a podcast called *The Breakfast Club*. In one episode, a statement jolted me: "Abundance is our birthright!" I had never heard such a proclamation that speaks of God's abundance as a birthright, but why not? So often, we behave as if our lives are not worth it. Jesus counters that notion and reminds us that we are created in the image of God. Rethinking is another way to shift into our assigned abundance. Like the disciples on that day of the greatest haul of fish and the value of listening, when we follow the instructions of Jesus, we can solve many human problems.

Questions for Reflection

1. What problem is God inviting you and others to solve?

2. What resources do you need?

3. What do you need to shift so that you can help others?

CHAPTER FIVE
Realigning Relationships

By Stephen Handy

Choose people who lift you up.
Michelle Obama

There are costs associated with the lack of alignment. For example, driving a car is an effective, efficient method of transportation until you hit a pothole and the alignment goes haywire. The wheels then pull one way or another. Unless you are a mechanic, you can ruin a good tire or two and put you and others at risk of a blowout at any time. Leaders can also get out of alignment and grow accustomed to malaise and unproductive behavior.

Jesus invited the disciples to cast the net to the other side, a different side, and it worked. Miraculously, more fish were caught than could be hauled in. The catch expanded their spiritual capacity to see and believe what was possible.

Follow the Instructions

As a student in elementary school, whenever I received a final grade, the teacher subtracted a point because I didn't follow instructions. Not following those simple instructions caused me to miss an "A" by just a few points. Often, I would try and convince the teacher that it was a simple oversight. Over time, I started to realize that following instructions has its reward. When we follow the instructions of Jesus, the response is greater than we can ever imagine. Paul the Apostle writes to the church and community in Ephesus: "Now all glory to God, who is able, through his mighty power at work within us, to accomplish infinitely more than we might ask or think" (Ephesians 3:20 NLT).

Jesus' instruction brings the disciples into alignment with a greater perspective and an abundance beyond what they could have ever imagined. Sometimes the way we view our assignment of ministry can interfere with our alignment with God's instruction. After the miracle of "the enormous catch," I often think about the disciples' initial feelings when this carpenter and Jewish rabbi named Jesus offered them another way to think. Don't we all need to examine our relationships? Shouldn't we desire to be among people who nudge us—or even those who push us—to a different point of view?

Or are we content with the myth of normal as limited self-expectations in our lives?

Realignment Could Save Our Lives

Typically, most people experience seasons of realignment. These seasons invite leaders to reexamine, reimagine, reorient, and even recalibrate their relationships. With reassessment, current relationships can be realigned. All relationships have a purpose and a timeline. No human relationship lasts forever. God does not send people into our lives to put us on pause but to activate something that is already in us. Jesus' actions instruct the disciples to think differently while inviting them to act accordingly as the Holy Spirit leads them. After Jesus' resurrection, it was normal behavior for the disciples to retreat and default to what they knew, whether it worked or not. Isn't the challenge for us as leaders to discover what we don't know?

Changes in perspective and behavior often don't happen until leaders hit a point of no return. Jesus awaits his disciples then and us today for that point of no return! We don't hear it enough, but leadership has a responsibility and an obligation to create a culture of shifting to an alternative way, especially when the business, nonprofit, school, or religious entity has stalled or retreated from the needs of people. No leader desires to stall or become numb to the changes necessary for cultural renewal, but it happens daily. Resistance to realignment happens over time. The disciples simply did what they knew to do because, in the past, their behavior produced the fish needed for their families and others.

Sometimes Realignment Comes from the Outside

Recently, I met with a group of CEOs and executive directors of nonprofits. As we engaged in conversation, it became obvious that their relational capacity was depleted. Most of these leaders felt a lack of trust, transparency, and belonging within their organizations. In a culture of metrics, leaders, if not careful, will be driven by measurements instead of by the value of deep and abiding relationships. Success is more than numbers in every field of human endeavor. Jesus' number one characteristic for leadership was a word and reality he modeled; he called it *relationships*. Nothing more, nothing less. If our working relationships are grounded in the toxicity of distrust, lack of communication, and disconnection, it will only produce misaligned ideas and misinformed strategies. However, when our mental health is linked to healthy relationships, then trust, transparency, and belonging are evident in the missional alignment with culture and people.

Jesus' disciples are experiencing deep and destructive trauma. Jesus' death has shaken them and others to the core of their very beings. Dr. Peter Levine, a psychotherapist and expert in trauma, explains that trauma is a common experience. Trauma is personal and often invisible. He notes that the effects of trauma can be barely perceptible or entirely debilitating and that these effects can be a stable part of someone's experience or surface intermittently because stress triggers them. "In short," he says, "trauma is about a loss of connection—to our bodies, to our families, to others, and to the world around us."[14] Trauma is collective, too. Large events, cultural practices, and the structure of organizations can cause trauma to be felt in entire groups of people.[15]

But after Jesus instructs the disciples to shift their mindset, they must be ready for the skillset shift. The disciples already possessed the skillset, but they needed a spiritual mind shift to move forward. Words can help leaders move forward differently, but the distraction of "different" calls and causes can prevent people from making the needed changes. Imagine if Jesus had said,

---

[14] Peter A. Levine, *Healing Trauma, A Pioneering Program for Restoring the Wisdom of Your Body*, (Sounds True, Incorporated, March 1, 2006).

[15] http://ldswomenproject.com/2021/01/man-of-sorrows-becoming-trauma-informed-in-the-body-of-christ.

"No! Don't worry, you guys are just stuck in the past with no ability or motivation to shift." However, the hope of this story is Jesus' words were enough to move them mentally, emotionally, relationally, and physically to a different place. All people experience trauma to varying degrees. However, few leaders seek assistance and secure the services of a therapist to guide them to self-discovery and the origins of their traumatic moments. After the miraculous haul of fish, the disciples don't see Jesus until his words open their eyes. Words matter, especially when we, as leaders, get stuck.

Jesus' Presence Gives Us Agency Alignment!

Agency is our ability to know and act as God gives us the privilege to choose. The disciples find themselves in spiritual limbo because the fish are not biting, and their Messiah is dead. Their old way of thinking isn't working anymore, and the invasion of COVID-19 for us today has proved that reality at all levels of leadership, regardless of your occupation or vocation. With his presence, Jesus awakens their innermost being. Before taking action, Jesus provokes the disciples' inner beings to move from the old to the new, from being consumed by the obstacles to seeing opportunity and imagining a way of being before doing. Leaders emerge and evolve from a clear sense of agency, not by performing but by spending time within. Our human agency is linked to the person of Christ and not to a program. Our being does not—and cannot—exist apart from God. Luke writes in **Acts 17:28 (NRSVUE):** "For 'In him we live and move and have our being'; as even some of your own poets have said, 'For we, too, are his offspring.'"

> *The disciple whom Jesus loved said to Peter, "It's the Lord." When Simon Peter heard that it was the Lord, he put back on the clothes that he had taken off and jumped into the sea. The other disciples came with the boat and dragged the net full of fish. They weren't far from the shore, only about 100 yards.*
>
> **John 21:7-8 (GOD'S WORD Translation)**

At some point in life, leaders need someone to remind them to pay attention to their behavior and encourage them to exercise self-examination. John, the beloved disciple, speaks into Peter's traumatic heart and jolts his soul after suggesting that this is the (and his) Lord. Never underestimate the negative and exhaustive dangers of trauma. Unresolved trauma can prevent the best of us from surfacing and can prevent humanity from flourishing. Simon Peter hears with his heart and puts back on his outer garments. By putting back on his clothes, Peter is committed to coming back to Christ. Recommitment is a key value for leaders, especially when it involves an organization's mission.

Mirrors Don't Lie!

Looking in the mirror offers the discipline of a great daily self-practice. Mirrors don't lie because they only reflect what is right in front of them, what's real, and what's now. Michael Jackson, the king of pop, recorded the song "Man in the Mirror," which was nominated for Song of the Year at the 31st Grammy Awards. The refrain is simple yet profound and challenging:

> *I'm starting with the man in the mirror*
> *I'm asking him to change his ways*
> *And no message could've been any clearer*
> *If they wanna make the world a better place*
> *Take a look at yourself and then make a change.*[16]

Have you ever questioned or denied what's in the mirror? I do it all the time. I think about what I want to look like at that particular time, whether in the morning or at night before bed. What can happen when looking in the mirror is a reverse sense of security. Instead of goodness and mercy, denial and delusion can become the illusions that prevent us from casting the nets—our purpose, perspectives, thoughts, and strategies—to the other side. God awaits us on the other side, or the other

---

[16] Michael Jackson, "Man in the Mirror," track 4 on Bad, Epic Records, 1988, vinyl.

half, of our lives. Peter is able and willing to confront his trauma, listen, and jump into the abundance of his future. But Peter, like everyone, needs help to liberate himself from his past pain and historical hurt. In an immediate mind shift, after hearing "It is the Lord," the balm of Christ, Peter desires to be with Jesus, so he jumps into the sea. Every stroke and step Peter takes brings him closer to Jesus, who, from the beginning, called him to simply "Follow me."

Humility Attracts Abundance!

Regaining alignment with Jesus takes courage, resilience, and humility. Leaders are taught to know everything and always be right. What happens when we lead by humility instead of desiring honor? Instead of seeking to be correct, Peter relinquishes his authority and models the value of resilient and redemptive behavior. As Peter is restoring his relationship with Jesus, he sees the value of communal relationships. The haul of fish is not for a chosen few; it is for the larger community and represents all those Jesus invites on the journey. This community was shocked by the unbelievable death of Jesus, their Savior. Maybe you have heard the leadership mantra, "Organizations rise or fall on leadership." On the contrary, John's gospel teaches us that obedience can lead us to dynamic results grounded in the redemptive and restorative acts of Jesus' words. Words matter, especially those from the Savior of the world.

All of us experience lapses in judgment. Peter reflects the reality of our humanness. Also, Peter has forgotten that Jesus, as the Kingdom on Earth, offers the concept of abundance. Jesus teaches that evil comes to kill, steal, and destroy, but he (Jesus) comes to invite us into a life of abundant living. For a moment, Peter finds himself in a mindset of scarcity until Jesus reminds him to cast the net to the other side where the fish are waiting. Scarcity is when we believe there isn't enough food, clothing, or housing. Most people believe God has created enough for everyone to have their fair or equitable share to ensure their basic needs are met.

Recently, I saw a great T-shirt that promoted the idea that abundance is our birthright. It called me to the biblical text in Genesis 25:29-34 (NRSVUE):

> *Once when Jacob was cooking a stew, Esau came in from the field, and he was famished. Esau said to Jacob, "Let me eat some of that red stuff, for I am famished!" (Therefore he was called Edom.) Jacob said, "First sell me your birthright." Esau said, "I am about to die; of what use is a birthright to me?" Jacob said, "Swear to me first." So he swore to him and sold his birthright to Jacob. Then Jacob gave Esau bread and lentil stew, and he ate and drank and rose and went his way. Thus Esau despised his birthright.*

Jacob was more reflective and contemplative, whereas Esau was more assertive and aggressive, which was favored by Isaac, his father. In a patriarchal society, men were defined by their assertive and aggressive nature. Anything less was considered weak and passive. As Esau returns from working in the field, he enters the house where Jacob has prepared a meal. Esau is willing to sell his birthright—his long-term blessings of a double portion of his inheritance—forfeit leading the family and give up judicial authority for short-term pleasure.

Neither brother understood that they both possessed God's abundance. Like these brothers, we need to understand the significance of realigning our relationships for the greater common good of our community, businesses, and congregations, not our personal gain. Leaders can't afford to compromise God's plans for their lives. Temptations, trials, and tests are always lurking around the corner. Resilient leaders think about and examine their relationships as a regular practice. Surrounding ourselves with others who are gifted beyond our capacity creates a culture of collective genius.

Jesus illustrates the "other side" mentality for his disciples in feeding the five thousand-plus people. Before that gathering, as the Passover Festival was approaching—a time to remember God's deliverance of the Israelites out of bondage—we see Jesus exhibiting his power by healing people. The disciples are front and center, watching as Jesus performs another miracle. A few moments later, the group of five thousand-plus follows Jesus to a hillside with deep hunger. I contend that this hunger was both physical and spiritual. Philip experiences anxiety about *how to* feed those people as opposed to *who will* feed these people.

Money is considered the barrier in most cases of hunger, but with Jesus, it's a mindset. Communities need two primary components to see the alternative, the other side. One is access to resources, and the other is exposure to different ways of thinking. Jesus offers both when feeding the five thousand-plus people. Andrew, Simon Peter's brother, notices a boy in the crowd with a brown bag lunch containing two fish and five barley loaves of bread. This boy's "Happy Meal" is about to become a holy meal feeding thousands. Do you still believe in miracles?

Years ago, McKendree decided to "give" its church building to the community by leveraging space for its unhoused neighbors and community partners. We were willing to shift our perspective of what a church building was designed for beyond worshiping God on Sunday, a mid-week Bible study, and committee meetings. After forming our nonprofit, Restoration

Pointe, which included a clothes closet, 5&2 weekly meal, and a transitional housing facility (The Foundry) for men, we needed major renovations done to the building. One of the local developers heard about our efforts to reduce homelessness in downtown Nashville and donated $50,000 for major repairs and replacements of appliances.

After praying for a way to offer affordable housing, we were able to partner with Metro Government of Nashville and another nonprofit called Community Care Fellowship and secured affordable housing after a 90-day stay in our facility. God's abundance never ceases, but leaders must be humble in that alignment. We needed to shift from a charity mindset to a justice model so that all of God's people could experience God's abundance, especially with the basic needs of food, clothing, and housing.

As the GOD'S WORD Translation of John 21:8 states, "The other disciples came with the boat and dragged the net full of fish." Overwhelmed by the blessings of multiplication, the other disciples and fishermen had to realign their physical relationships to ensure that the net full of fish was brought to the shore and secured so that everyone could eat. What is possible when we work together and do not focus on ourselves? What happens when we go fishing with the hope of catching enough so that our family can eat, and there is an encounter with God's presence? It's a calling to a collaborative community.

Collaborative Tables

When God's people invite the community of businesses, governments, nonprofits, and faith communities to the table to collaborate on the reality of scarcity, poverty, homelessness, healthcare, and other disparities, many of our societal ills can be eradicated. This process of table inclusion demands an invitation to diverse people and voices in and around the community where God has placed our "boats," businesses, governments, nonprofits, and communities.

Living in a western culture where individualism is the order of the day, one's restrictive culture can be a deterrent "to filling the nets of resources" if we allow only one way, one side, to order and sustain our planning and strategies for success. Defining success by one person, one perspective is dangerous and short-lived. When leaders share in the visioning and planning process, we also share in the prosperity and become a more equitable society. Jesus challenges Peter and the other disciples to reexamine their traditions of rightness and one-way-ness. Requesting Jesus show us another way only adds to the abundance that awaits our churches, companies and communities.

Jesus answers us with a way to experience abundance: cast on the right or other side. After the miraculous catch, others were waiting to assist with the (re)distribution of the witnessed abundance. What if we could think about relationships as assets, something of heavenly value in the eyes of God? Beyond money, the greatest resource is being in relationship with people. Businesses, nonprofits, and governmental agencies thrive when people are considered valued assets necessary for maintaining alignment on the journey. Mark Zuckerberg created Facebook as a sophomore at Harvard to connect students on campus, which was a realignment of how he viewed and valued relationships. Today, Facebook is the largest social media platform. His "fishing net" has over 2.9 billion monthly active users.[17] Don't underestimate the value of shifting. Changing lenses creates a view from the balcony, not merely from the ground floor.

Now, with a new set of lenses, think about how everyone you meet is made in the image and likeness of God. Yes, I said *everyone*. Fishing is similar to discipleship. Both have a place where fish or people gather in nature, whether on land or in water. Both have bait for catching fish or connecting with others.

---

[17] https://blog.hootsuite.com/facebook-statistics/.

One involves what attracts certain fish, and the other engages diverse people in different ways. Both involve patience and awareness that if you are not catching or engaging, you must have the courage and faith to change your method, strategy, or position so you can catch and engage. Using only one way to connect with others will not engage everyone. Discipleship emerges in and through authentic, trusting relationships. When we are willing to align ourselves with the principles, practices, and patterns of Jesus and the desires of God, we will experience abundance beyond our imagination and capacity to handle it.

Questions for Reflection

1. In this day and age, how might you explore different types of relationships that are currently missing from your relationship pool?

2. Based on categories of resilience and humility, how might you, as a leader, start to think more broadly about realigning the relationships within your personal life, work, and community?

CHAPTER SIX

Reevaluating Stewardship

By Mike Bowie

*If you want something new,
you have to stop doing something old.*

Peter F. Drucker

If the unexpected disruption of the pandemic taught us anything, it taught us that we need to be good stewards of our resources. During the early stages of the pandemic, we experienced a shortage of basic necessities, such as toilet paper and bottled water. As people began hoarding toilet paper, we received a wake-up call about the importance of being good stewards of such a simple product. When I speak of stewardship, I'm referring to being a capable manager of one's resources—even something as common as toilet paper.

A practical understanding of stewardship is that everything we possess belongs to the Lord. We see this perspective of stewardship in the disciples, for after they began following Jesus, they were clear: Caesar was no longer Lord. Jesus was Lord! They now understood the expectations and responsibilities that came with being people of The Way.

In John 21:10-12 (NIV), we're told:

> *Jesus said to them, "Bring some of the fish you have just caught." So Simon Peter climbed back into the boat and dragged the net ashore. It was full of large fish, one-hundred-fifty-three, but even with so many the net was not torn. Jesus said to them, "Come and have breakfast." None of the disciples dared ask him, "Who are you?" They knew it was the Lord.*

In this passage of Scripture, we witness stewardship happening in real time. After the disciples catch the fish, Jesus says, give me what you have. He is teaching the disciples the importance of giving what they possess first to him, and he would take what they gave him and transform it.

I know there have been times that I haven't given what I've earned to God first. Far too often, we are tempted to hold on to what we have earned because we've worked hard for it. Although the disciples fished all night, Jesus wanted them to realize that *he* gave them the ability to work all night and bring in an amazing catch. For anyone reading this, even if you've worked hard earning your degrees and are now an executive member of the "C-suite," remember that God gave you the ability to obtain the success you currently enjoy.

Now, leaders must be good stewards of their time, talent, and treasure and also be good managers regarding their creativity, innovation, and imagination. This new perspective is not an "either/or" situation but a "both/and" reality. As resources continue to decrease, it's imperative that innovation increase. And by *innovation*, I mean this: what creative methods are we implementing as the body of Christ to ensure that, as good stewards, everyone's essential needs are met? And further, as the nation becomes more economically, politically, and racially divided, what can we do to make sure the needs of "the least of these," who Jesus referred to in Matthew 25:36-40, are met?

A Practical Understanding of Stewardship

Jesus tells the disciples to bring what they have caught to him so it can be blessed. The fish the disciples caught weren't just for their own consumption; their bounty was meant to be shared and to bless others in need. This blessing went beyond them. The disciples were blessed to be a blessing to others. I believe that here in this experience, Jesus was reminding the disciples—and even us today—that whatever we catch or possess, we must give it to him first so it can also be a blessing to others. This concept is reiterated in Psalm 24:1: "The earth is the LORD's, and everything in it, the world, and all who live in it" (NIV). In essence, Jesus is taking cues from his ancestor David and reminding us all that everything we have first belongs to God. This perspective is critical because we know our giving to God can lead to a life of abundance while withholding from God can lead to a life of scarcity.

Could it be that we have struggled with issues of lack and scarcity because we have failed to think about others and give to God first what belongs to God? *Now, if you can't say amen, say OUCH-man!*

I can say definitively that the disruption of the pandemic has taught me that everything I have, everything I own, really belongs to God. While that's not a profound statement, I think it needs to be revisited, for I truly believe that most things that happen in the world—from mass incarceration, climate change, and abject poverty to physical illness—are a matter of stewardship.

As we look at the lives of the disciples, we see they were intentional about being faithful witnesses and good stewards of their resources. This witness was evident, for whenever they went fishing, it was a given that regardless of whoever caught the fish, the fish wasn't just for that person individually but, rather, for everyone collectively. Jesus made this clear when he asked the disciples to give him the fish to cook breakfast. When one person ate, others connected in community would eat as well. Stewardship wasn't about what they could keep for themselves. It was about what they could give away to meet every kingdom need.

However, as Jesus reminds us, stewardship is far more than financial resources or tangible items.

In my denomination, as directed by our *Book of Discipline*, when a person becomes a professing member of a United Methodist congregation, they profess their faith in God, their desire to live as disciples of Jesus Christ, and their commitment to join with a church community to keep the vows and their baptismal covenant. They also agree to faithfully participate in the church's ministries with "their prayers, their presence, their gifts, their service, and their witness" and "to receive and profess the Christian faith as contained in the Scriptures of the Old and New Testaments."[18] It's a holistic approach to stewardship: stewardship of self (heart), of personal resources (time, talent), and of everything we possess (finances).

---

[18] *The Book of Discipline of The United Methodist Church – 2016* (The United Methodist Publishing House, 2016), paragraph 217.6-7, 2016.

While Jesus is speaking of fish in this chapter, the stewardship he's truly highlighting is the stewardship of witness. As we continue to navigate this season of disruption, it's extremely important that, like never before, followers of Jesus become good stewards—not just of our financial gifts but also by our witness. The Rev. Mark W. Stamm, the author of the Discipleship Ministries resource *Our Membership Vows* and professor of Christian worship at Perkins School of Theology, states that the term *witness* means "to highlight the mission and evangelistic responsibilities of church membership. It also reminds United Methodists to live out their vows publicly. Churches need to discern locally how they are going to do that in a specific way and a specific place."[19]

When I think about being good stewards of our witness, I'm reminded of one of my favorite stories in the Gospel of John: Jesus feeding five thousand hungry men, plus women and children (John 6:1-14). When faced with this overwhelming task, Andrew asks a little boy to give him his lunch, which comprises two fish and five loaves of bread. Now, that boy could have kept his lunch for himself, but maybe he knew the most important truth: when we give our possessions first to God, we

---

[19] https://www.umc.org/en/content/what-it-means-to-witness-honoring-our-united-methodist-vow.

activate abundance in our lives. We know that when Jesus received the boy's lunch, he broke the bread and gave thanks, and then God multiplied the small lunch and transformed it into a massive buffet. Here, Jesus was basically providing a free master class on giving, reminding the disciples that when you give what may seem like a little into the hands of God first, God can multiply it into much. On that day, scholars believe more than fifteen thousand people were fed with one boy's lunch, and there were twelve baskets of leftovers.

The basic principle evident here is if you are willing to give your best to God, you will not only have what you need, but you will have more to bless others in need—and even twelve baskets of leftovers available for your ministry. But to get to this place, God is challenging you to become better stewards of your witness.

Stewardship of Witness

Now you're probably asking what this has to do with being a good steward of our witness. Let's make an abrupt shift—pun intended—and explore why more than fifteen thousand hungry people gathered there in the first place. Could it be that Jesus caught them at lunchtime and everyone was hungry? Or perhaps there was heightened food insecurity, and it created a food desert in their community. Grappling with this question, I've often wondered whether a food crisis began when disciples shifted their allegiance from Caesar to Jesus. When the disciples confessed Jesus as Lord, I believe it had immediate negative consequences—repercussions regarding their basic need for food. As we look at fifteen thousand hungry people in a remote area where no stores are available, it's no different than the food deserts present in urban and rural communities throughout America today.

What is a food desert? According to the U.S. Department of Agriculture, there are many ways to define a food desert and measure access to food. The USDA's Economic Research Service says a *food desert* is defined as low-income census tracts with a substantial number of residents with little access to retail outlets selling healthy and affordable foods. A *census tract* is a small, relatively permanent county subdivision that usually contains between one thousand to eight thousand people but generally averages around four thousand. Census tracts qualify as food deserts if they meet low-income and low-access thresholds. *Low income* is considered a poverty rate of 20 percent or greater or a median family income at or below 80 percent of the statewide or metropolitan area median family income. *Low access* is when at least five hundred persons and/

or at least 33 percent of the population lives more than a mile from a supermarket or large grocery store (or ten miles, in the case of rural census tracts).[20]

Currently, an estimated 13.5 million people in the United States have low access to a supermarket or large grocery store, with 82 percent of them living in urban areas, according to data from the 2000 Census of Population and Housing.[21]

Supermarkets and large grocery stores are defined as food stores with at least two million dollars in annual sales and containing all the major food departments.[22] Unfortunately, some low-income communities in the United States lack stores that sell healthy, affordable food. The lack of store access in these communities contributes to poor diet, obesity, and other diet-related illnesses.

Given all this, we can see that in a very real sense, there was a census tract evident on this mountainside in Galilee where Jesus encountered fifteen thousand hungry people. And through his compassion for justice, concern for the poor, and connection to his heavenly father, there

---

[20] https://www.ers.usda.gov/data-products/food-access-research-atlas/documentation/#definitions.

[21] U.S. Department of Agriculture report. https://www.ers.usda.gov/data-products/food-access-research-atlas/documentation/.

[22] https://www.ers.usda.gov/data-products/foot-environment-atlas/documentation.

was no longer a scarcity of food. Not only did access to food decrease, but hope and possibilities increased.

Charity vs. Justice

As followers of Jesus, we must become better stewards of our witness to address the prevalent food deserts in underserved and marginalized communities. I call this "stewardship of justice." Now, when I speak of being stewards of justice, I'm not just referring to feeding hungry people but also—and just as importantly—to becoming prophetic voices in addressing the lack of supermarkets willing to invest in low-income communities. It's time for passionate servant leaders of Jesus to intentionally hold corporations accountable for their unwillingness to be good stewards of their witness and eliminate food deserts.

It's the responsibility of the body of Christ to broaden its witness and perspective of justice. Many churches have settled for providing food pantries and community gardens. While those are good efforts, we must seek to widen our witness beyond charity. Charity is the act of providing temporary provisions for others. While it provides temporary relief, it doesn't address the root cause of the problem. Justice, however, is permanent. The church must not only give people fish but begin to equip and empower the people to fish for themselves.

One of my mentors, Dr. Zan Wesley Holmes, unpacks the difference between charity and justice. In his book *Encountering Jesus*, he says a good example of charity is the parable of the Good Samaritan. The Samaritan provided the man clothing for his nakedness, bandages for his wounds, and monetary provisions for temporary shelter at an inn—all charity. However, as Holmes says, justice goes beyond temporary housing with a practical yet powerful example. Justice goes a step further into the parable, addressing the root cause of highway robbery, exploring ways to provide better security measures to prevent highway robberies in the future, and implementing reform efforts for the robbers—or better employment opportunities for would-be robbers.[23]

In this example, Dr. Holmes provides a blueprint and strategy for a vital, impactful congregation. If the church seeks to revitalize its congregation and transform its community in this disruption, it must enhance and embrace the stewardship of justice. Being stewards of justice could be the prophetic witness needed to address hunger and end food deserts.

Churches seeking innovative ways to engage their communities must experience a shift from being private

---

[23] Zan Wesley Holmes, *Encountering Jesus* (Abingdon Press, March 1, 1998).

to public in how they witness to others. This shift requires leaving the comfort we may feel within the four walls of the sanctuary and intentionally engaging in the life of the surrounding community. Not only are we compelled to go beyond the four walls, but we are further called to access and discern the needs and injustices hindering our communities from prospering.

Mark W. Stamm, the author of *Our Membership Vows*, suggests that before we proceed beyond those walls, we must first remember that our baptismal vows call each of us to resist evil and repent of our sin and commit to resisting and working against injustice and oppression.[24] Therefore, we must prayerfully ask, What are the current injustices plaguing my community? What do oppression and injustice look like, and do I possess the courage to name these evils?

This shift in perspective and behavior takes courage, holy boldness, and resilience.

Ministries of Justice

Emory Fellowship in Washington, D.C., pastored by Dr. Joe W. Daniels, Jr., is a great example of an effective witness and steward of justice. Emory United

---

[24] Mark W. Stamms, *Our Membership Vows in the United Methodist Church* (Upper Room, May 4, 2015).

Methodist Church was once a dying congregation, but Dr. Daniels helped the church become a model for church revitalization and community transformation. Dr. Daniels is a visionary and prophetic leader who has demonstrated what a dynamic, creative, and innovative ministry entails. Emory's story parallels Jesus' feeding the multitude with two fish and five loaves.

Although the membership of Emory Fellowship isn't considered "mega-sized," the congregation possesses a "mega vision" for the community. Unlike the disciples' initial response, Dr. Daniels and Emory chose not to turn the hurting, homeless, and hungry away in their community. Instead, they shifted their witness from private to public. This pivot became a reality when they embraced the acronym REAL, consistently seeking to be Relevant, Enthusiastic, Authentic, and Loving. The idea of being REAL compelled Emory Fellowship to be effective witnesses who strive to be good stewards of justice versus simply settling to provide charity. Their understanding of justice fostered a prophetic vision at Emory that continues to revitalize and transform the congregation and the community.

Dr. Daniels' witness and vision for Emory couldn't come to pass without initially assessing the power that existed in the community. It couldn't evolve by doing ministry on the left side. (Again, remember, this is not a political term.) Now, you must understand, Dr. Daniels didn't dwell on the small size of Emory's membership. Instead, he focused on the power of all the assets before him.

In the Scripture for this chapter, John 21:9-12, the disciples failed to be effective witnesses because they focused on the size of the small lunch and failed to recognize the size of the powerful Savior right in front of them. How often do we do that? We get so focused on what we don't have, and we fail to give our attention to God, who makes much out of little. When we fail to give our attention to God, it hinders our witness, and we ultimately find ourselves settling to provide convenient charity instead of digging deeper to be good stewards of justice.

Emory skillfully enacts justice in its community by assessing available power and cultivating strategic partnerships. In his book *The Power of Real: Changing Lives, Changing Churches, Changing Communities*, Dr. Daniels suggests that before we attempt to engage in our community, we must understand its power dynamics. He states three sectors—private, government, and public— must be present to experience effective community development. Amazing things happen when these three sectors are present and aligned with the congregation's vision. Further, Daniels believes the church should not just sit on the sidelines and spectate; the church needs to be a major player and participate in the public, private, and governmental sectors as an organizer and catalyst for community transformation.[25]

Emory Fellowship exemplifies the power of possessing a prophetic witness and embodying a stewardship of justice. As a result of its right-side vision, the church has launched a $55-million community development project that provides employment opportunities, affordable housing, and, even more so, hope to a once hopeless community.

Another ministry that demonstrates prophetic witness and stewardship of justice is Crossroads United Methodist Church. Pastored by the Rev. Dr. Adrienne Zackery since 2016, Crossroads is a 30-year-old congregation in Compton, California, located in the southern part of Los Angeles County. The city's population diversity breaks down to 69.3 percent Hispanic or Latino, 27.1 percent African American, 1.0 percent white, and 1.5 percent of other descent.[26] In 2019, "The city violent crime rate for Compton was higher than the national violent crime rate average by 201.09 percent.[27] In the early 2000s, gangs, drugs, and violence were synonymous with Compton.

---

[25] Joseph W. Daniels, Jr., *The Power of Real: Changing Lives, Changing Churches, Changing Communities* (Fun and Done Press, September 9, 2011).

[26] https://www.census.gov/quickfacts/comptoncitycalifornia.

[27] https://www.cityrating.com/crime-statistics/california/compton.html.

In 2016, Dr. Zackery first got involved with prison ministry because she had incarcerated family members. Out of this pain, she took a team to the Strengthening the Black Church for 21st Century (SBC21) National Prison Summit in Dallas, Texas, and it changed the trajectory of her life and ministry. Initially, she encountered resistance from some in her congregation who feared getting involved in this mission. To overcome this hurdle, Crossroads United Methodist Church began a Bible study called "See All the People" by the late Junius Dotson. Through this discipleship teaching series, members became supportive advocates for this new mission.

Out of pain, God ignited a passion for formerly incarcerated persons. Crossroads UMC cultivated strategic partnerships and began engaging in the community by helping people get their criminal records expunged. The church has developed the Karen Henry Expungement Clinic and assisted over eleven hundred people with criminal record clearances.

One inspirational story from the expungement process is about a young woman named Hope (talking about a perfect name for a problematic situation). In 2017, a relative referred Hope to the Expungement Clinic at Crossroads. Growing up, Hope got hooked on drugs, signed fraudulent checks, and was convicted of fourteen criminal offenses. After encountering Crossroads UMC, Hope's life was transformed. She stopped using drugs and started to look for gainful employment. Hope was hired as a secretary of a loan company and was later promoted to executive assistant. Through the expungement clinics, family reunification, and homeless ministries at Crossroads, Hope and others disproportionally impacted by the criminal justice and social systems are given hope.

Crossroads also participates in partnerships with the City of Compton, the Department of Children and Family Services, Shields for Families, the Veterans Association, and other faith and nonprofit organizations.

With its reimagined mission, the Crossroads vision has evolved and expanded its homeless ministry to include a supportive housing development project called "Blake at Crossroads Compton." This multi-use development will include fifty to sixty housing apartment units, a worship sanctuary, a multipurpose center, a commercial kitchen, and administrative offices.

Crossroads is a great example of a congregation that is intentional about its prophetic witness for Jesus Christ to marginalized, oppressed people and for embodying the stewardship of justice. Today, with the notoriety of Dr. Dre, Serena and Venus Williams, and Kendrick

Lamar, a renaissance is happening in this community. Crossroads has shifted from givers of charity to advocates for justice. Without question, healing, health, and hope are coming STRAIGHT OUTTA COMPTON! (I couldn't wait to say that!)

Food, hygiene kits, diapers, and backpacks have been given to hundreds of people who are unsheltered and food insecure. The church sponsors COVID vaccination clinics and LGBQTI support groups. Also, vocational training classes and job placement are provided.

Finally, another congregation with a prophetic public witness that has enacted justice to meet the needs of the least, last, and left-out is St. John's Church in downtown Houston, led by two of my mentors, Dr. Rudy and Juanita Rasmus. St. John's epitomizes the embodiment of being stewards of justice. As I mentioned in an earlier chapter, St. John's operates with a right-side mindset, and since 1992, this congregation has taken risks and engaged in ministry that has been uncertain, uncommon, and uncomfortable. From the beginning, they have chosen to give hope to those who are addicted and those infected with HIV and to be a ministry that intentionally accepts and loves *all* people. Taking this stance hasn't been popular, and it has also been messy. I say "messy" because this ministry compels people to serve those who may have personal hygiene issues or mental health challenges, and it forces them to love people for who they are, not for what they have.

St. John's Church chose to become a faithful steward of justice for one key reason: justice was the focal point of Jesus' ministry. This focus on justice gets to the root of what I've discovered while following Jesus: justice wasn't just what Jesus *did*; justice was *who Jesus was*!

I'm reminded of a specific occasion in the Gospel of John when justice appears in a moment of messiness. When the Pharisees caught the woman committing adultery, they sought to execute "justice" on the spot:

> *"Teacher, this woman was caught in the act of adultery. In the Law Moses commanded us to stone such women. Now what do you say?" They were using this question as a trap, in order to have a basis for accusing him. But Jesus bent down and started to write on the ground with his finger. When they kept on questioning him, he straightened up and said to them, "Let any one of you who is without sin be the first to throw a stone at her."*
>
> **John 8:4-7 (NIV)**

Aren't you glad that justice stepped in and said yes when folks counted you out? Aren't

you grateful that justice stepped in and gave you a chance when people said you weren't qualified? Right now, I dare you to stop and praise God for justice that forged a path for you when you couldn't see a way.

For more than thirty years, St. John's has been committed to flawed, forsaken, and forgotten people. Their "ministry to the messy" has developed more than $60 million in housing for the homeless, hope for the forsaken, and help for the hopeless. Although this ministry has never had an abundance of financial resources, it has possessed a wealth of strategic partnerships through St. John's 501(c)(3) nonprofit Bread of Life. This nonprofit has provided the resources to generate kingdom revenue to meet the community's needs for "the least of these."

If you seek to curate additional revenue, maybe God is calling you to create a nonprofit committed to bringing healing, help, and hope to the least, last, and left-out. Perhaps you are doubting or questioning your ministry ability or capacity, but maybe God is challenging you to shift your witness and embody a stewardship of justice focused on loving flawed, forsaken, and forgotten people.

If you are facing a crisis, as the disciples did in meeting the needs of fifteen thousand hungry people, I dare you to shift. I dare you to trust Jesus with "the impossible."

People of Justice

I contend that if we seek to revitalize our congregations and transform our communities, we must become people of justice committed to repairing the brokenness prevalent in our communities. In Isaiah 58:12, the prophet challenges the Israelites to become "repairers of the breach." This is a message for us, too. Amidst so much uncertainty in our world, communities, and churches, God is looking for a generation of disrupters committed to repairing the brokenness in every area of life.

Canadian author Malcolm Gladwell says disrupters are creative, conscientious, and crazy. I agree with Gladwell and believe that during this season of disruption, God is seeking a generation of creative, conscientious, and crazy people who are willing to BOLDY stand in these gaps and challenge the powers that be who have created these wealth, health, and education gaps prevalent in so many underserved communities.

Churches are challenged like never before to begin demanding justice. We must demand economic justice, ensuring the creation of pro-labor, anti-poverty, and anti-racist policies to provide economic liberation for all people. We must also demand educational justice, ensuring every child receives access to high-quality, well-funded public education. In addition, we must demand healthcare justice that is universal, transparent, and equitable for all.

Then we must demand criminal justice reform that addresses the continuing inequalities in the system for Black, Brown, and poor White people. We must demand justice and fight against the proliferation of gun violence. And finally, we must demand justice for equal voting rights, women's rights, LGBTQI+ rights, labor rights, religious freedom rights, and immigrant rights.

Are we doing this? As we continue to face many injustices during these challenging times, are we being faithful stewards of justice? As a repairer of the breach, what area is God calling you or your ministry to engage in? Is it writing letters to your elected public officials asking them to enact new legislation to reduce unjust criminal sentences for those living in underserved communities? Maybe God is calling your congregation to empower the community through voting and participation in the democratic process. I believe every congregation—specifically Black congregations—must emphasize the important, sacred right of voting. Could God be calling your congregation or organization to adopt a local school to help disrupt the pipeline to prison?

Leaders in the church and leaders of corporations must make a drastic right-side shift in their witness and gain a new understanding regarding the stewardship of justice. As the late business philosopher Peter Drucker once said, "If you want something new, you have to stop doing something old."

Today, I dare you to shift your public witness and become a faithful steward of justice.

Questions for Reflection

1. Has there ever been a time when you needed a second chance, and someone gave it to you?

2. Have you ever given a second chance to someone else or helped forge a path for them when they couldn't see a way through a crisis?

3. What injustices are currently plaguing your community?

4. What might you do to help bring justice to the marginalized in your community?

5. Is your church involved in social justice issues? If not, how do you envision your church getting involved to bring hope and justice to the broken, forsaken, and forgotten people?

CHAPTER SEVEN

Recapturing/Reclaiming Discipleship

By Stephen Handy

Discipleship is the process of growing in God's love and life, so that we may enjoy and share the great news of salvation, making more disciples among our people.

Rabbi Sam Nedler

Jesus came, took the bread and gave it to them, and did the same with the fish. This was now the third time Jesus appeared to his disciples after he was raised from the dead

(John 21:13-14 NIV).

Discipleship is a process and practice, not a program. It is a process of becoming more Christlike by living into the patterns, practices, and behaviors of Jesus while extending love and grace to others. For many people, being a disciple means reading the Bible, praying daily, attending church, and maybe participating in an occasional mission trip. However, Jesus defines discipleship as being sent, sent into the neighborhood, the community, and the world as an immersion experience. Another understanding of discipleship is being in a relationship with Jesus and others so that we share a meal with someone and hear a story of hope and healing as wholeness emerges.

Eating together is a therapeutic, spiritual practice that restores the soul. Jesus captured the imaginations and hope of people around a simple table. Without eating, we become weak and are easily distracted from sharing who we are and what we have every day. At the table, not only do we say grace over the meal, but we also receive grace in the stories and conversations. Growing up, one of the intentional practices of my family was eating together at the dinner table. Sharing about our day—what we learned in school, our friendships, homework assignments, and grades—was always part of the conversation. Laughter, love, and hope were features of the invisible menu. Prayers were taught and recited at the table. Forgiveness and faith were exchanged. Healing of our brokenness emerged at the tables where our family and friends gathered. Honor, respect, and history were parts of the three-course meal every evening.

People invited Jesus to their tables. He invited himself to tables and even kicked over tables, and ultimately, he spent his last few moments around a table in an upper room with leaders, leaders who were part of a revolution of love, a shifting to the right or other side mindset.

Jesus spent his time eating and drinking—a lot of his time. He was a party animal. His mission strategy was a long meal that stretched into the evening. He did evangelism and disciples round a table with some grilled fish, a loaf of bread, and a pitcher of wine.[28]

If you think about it, Jesus spent more time around tables than he did in the temple. Why? Jesus was equipping leaders, building a model for discipleship that, in its purest form, is relational. Discipleship doesn't happen organically in institutional settings but in moments in the marketplace and with the marginalized. Sitting at tables allows us to make eye contact, sense the vibe of the other person's agency, and show gratitude for being in the same space together. Recapturing and reclaiming that space at the table can compel and then propel us to share stories of hope.

Sometimes leaders find themselves at the wrong table. Recently, I heard someone say, "If you are not at the table, you are probably on the menu." Some of the most complex tables to sit at begin in elementary and

---

[28] Tim Chester, A Meal with Jesus: *Discovering Grace, Community, and Mission around the Table* (Wheaton, Illinois, 2011), 13.

middle schools. Relationships are formed, and if you do not fit a certain profile, you can end up at the wrong table. Growing up in Nashville, my parents thought putting us in a Catholic school was a good idea, so we integrated the elementary school. During an initial recess, it was apparent that some of the boys didn't think I belonged in their school. I wasn't Catholic, White, or privileged. Immediately, it was clear that certain students were not familiar with "my type" around their table. This environment didn't align with what I was taught about discipleship. Where was the love expressed to me as a stranger in a foreign land? Where was the embracing of my person in a majority cultural context?

Trauma is real and gets disrupted when love is compromised by fear of "the other." Over a lifetime, all people experience trauma. Most people haven't recognized it, or they've suppressed it into their being. One day on the soccer field—which I was unfamiliar with growing up—I scored a goal, and someone yelled the "N" word. Hearing that word caused deep levels of trauma. We never heard that word in our house. Unfortunately, my initial reaction was to fight, so I did. After weeks of difficult conversations and tough recess sessions, I reclaimed my identity. Over time, people unlike me recognized that my humanity mattered, and we all became friends. As a disciple of Jesus, or whatever your faith community, no one ever gets to define us. For me, at my divine creation, God identified me as fully human and divine.

People are always looking for two things in this life: belonging and intimacy. Belonging is a natural aspect of human nature, whether it's in our congregations, family, school, or workplace. And the other bookend for humans is intimacy, and it's more for the soul. Both belonging and intimacy originate with God and are expressed in the life and love of Jesus. Jesus understands our desire and need for community, especially in times of loss. As a loved one transitions from this earthly place, there is a deep void of human presence in our hearts. That void of loss never goes away, but God (or a higher power) gives us the ability to endure and become strengthened as a result of our discipleship mindset in our relationship with others.

We are designed for relational discipleship and communion with Jesus and one another, and we are drawn to each other for belonging and intimacy. This communion is essential to our physical wellness and welfare. Years ago, while preparing to offer Holy Communion on Sunday, I reminded our congregation that maybe we needed to consider taking Communion every Sunday. There is something in us that desires more of God, and the sacrament of Communion is often limited to a monthly experience. I never understood why we restrict the frequency of Holy Communion when it is a means of grace that draws us into a closer, more meaningful relationship with God. Soon after discussing our need for more intimacy with God, we started to offer Communion every Sunday. One Sunday, a child walked down the aisle to take Communion by intinction (when we dip the bread into the cup). She received the bread, dipped it into the Communion cup, and then ate it. Immediately, she stopped and yelled, "I want more!" I thought, From the mouths of babes. She reminded all of us that we should desire more of Christ and more love, grace, and mercy.

The death of Jesus shook Peter and the disciples; they felt abandoned. Jesus' death got in the way of them seeing him again and being in communion with Jesus and even with each other. What gets in the way of your communion with God and others? Distractions and disappointments are natural daily occurrences that claim our attention and time. Sometimes we can't see the obvious, especially when Jesus reveals himself to us in a variety of ways.

FedEx's logo has a subtle arrow located intentionally within it to reinforce the company's promise to its customers. The company's mantra is simple and clear: "When it absolutely, positively needs to be there overnight!" After spending several minutes looking at the FedEx logo, I still couldn't find the arrow until someone pointed it out to me.

For no good reason, I just didn't see. My idea or preconceived notion of where the arrow should be differed from where the arrow was positioned in the logo.

Businesses, nonprofits, governmental agencies, and faith community leaders must see the alignment of their daily actions and experiences with their mission as an integrated process. As followers of Jesus—then and now—we are given a mission: "Go and make disciples of Jesus Christ." And now, due to missional drift, we need to recapture and reclaim discipleship. Nowadays, discipleship is often taught in a series of classes, but Jesus taught discipleship in the marketplace and through immersion experiences and stories, also known as parables.

In her book *Gospel Discipleship: 4 Pathways for Christian Discipleship*, Michelle J. Morris offers a research-based perspective on building a culture of pathways for discipleship. After examining each gospel and sending-forth message from Jesus, she suggests that we should recognize the distinctive DNA of each disciple's ability instead of seeing discipleship as monolithic or one-dimensional. Indeed, the gospel writers represent parts and parcels of a disciple. From Markan (Holy Spirit centered), Matthean (action driven), Lukan (relationship focused), and Johannine (mentor-apprentice nurtured) to the collective, each gospel writer offers a framework and footprints toward a more expansive means to discipleship and creating a discipleship culture.[29]

That's the alternative worth pursuing. It moves us away from the one-size-fits-all model of discipleship and allows for a contextualized approach within the marketplace so that people can connect to how they are designed by God to follow Jesus. In essence, with this approach, no one becomes indoctrinated with the generic dosage of discipleship; everyone is introduced to a specific way of discipleship that aligns with their life and individual strengths and abilities.

---

[29] Michelle J. Morris, Gospel Discipleship: *4 Pathways for Christian Discipleship* (Abingdon Press, March 31, 2020).

Each person is different—not better, but a unique part of the body of Christ. Even in business, teams are represented by different cultures, practices, and patterns of behavior that complement one another. Then and now, Jesus extends to everyone daily opportunities to claim or reclaim their identity in Christ. Segments of society like businesses, governments, and nonprofits might refer to this as claiming or reclaiming their core mission.

Several years ago, as I served on the executive board of the General Commission on Religion and Race and the CORR Action Fund, we awarded a grant to Vilma J. Cruz, pastor at LaPlaza United Methodist Church in downtown Los Angeles who reimagined discipleship with an initiative called "God is in the Graffiti: A New Lens on Religious Symbols in Street Art." This initiative provided a safe space and opportunity for ten young, unknown, urban graffiti artists to emerge as a community "changing leaders and disciples for prophetic ministry" by using visual art media (graffiti) and discerning relevant social issues for their community "through Christ-like models of Justice, Integrity and Excellence."

The "God is in the Graffiti" project provided this local church an opportunity and venue to invite and connect with and respond to the challenges of reaching new young people by being supportive of them, their crafts, and their interpretation of the text through art. By allowing young people to publicly express their perspectives on social and spiritual ideas, what evolved was a space in which their perspectives and practices were given larger margins to develop a much-needed out-of-the-box approach. Each participant offered different expressions intimately related to the ways the group fulfilled the call to be passionate and effective witnesses of Jesus Christ.

Peter and the other disciples head to the shore where Jesus awaits them with an unannounced meal that will awaken their souls. It is interesting how what they were trying to catch—fish—Jesus had already prepared. Is Jesus offering the disciples a way to rethink discipleship?

Table Setting and Sharing

Jesus came, took the bread and gave it to them, and did the same with the fish.

John 21:13 (NIV)

At the center of Jesus' ministry were experiences around the table sharing meals with others. In this case, however, Jesus is not being served; he is the one serving his disciples. Eating invites an appointment with the Holy Spirit, known as an "Aha" moment for the disciples. Bread is served, and fish is offered. Communion is happening. There isn't a formal liturgy, just Jesus hanging out with his friends, sharing life over meals. Maybe in that moment, the collective memories of the disciples were disrupted so that each one could remember and reengage with what Jesus promised: a return as proof of his Sovereignty. Jesus sets a table of grace that emphasizes second chances, and we celebrate this reality every time we see hands take the loaf and tear it apart.[30]

Time and time again, people need periods of re-engagement. It's in our nature to lose sight of our priorities. At the core of any connection or reconnection is the establishment of relationships. Jesus is the master of all types of relationships, even those prohibited by cultural laws, norms, and mores. If you want to form a relationship with someone, don't invite them to church first. Jesus didn't. Jesus met people in the marketplace and often invited them to a table where stories were told. It was there that forgiveness, redemption, and restoration happened.

Living in communion is the promise with Jesus. Leaders need communion to stay physically,

---

[30] Cynthia M. Campbell and Christine Coy Fohr, *Meeting Jesus at the Table* (Louisville, Kentucky: Westminster John Knox Press, 2023), 106.

emotionally, socially, and spiritually fit so they can build community. Community life doesn't happen without real, lived experiences with God and others. Evidence is required for communion and community to be integrated. Peter and the disciples participated in the movement of God's kingdom coming "on earth as it is in heaven" until Jesus died. Then there was a movement away from communion and community, intimacy and inclusiveness, trust and transparency to isolation and self.

Understanding the value of communion and community drives us to the movement of relationships. Everyone knows relationships come with costs, one of which is the loss of comfort. Humans desire comfort. When Peter and the disciples expect a comfortable life with their Savior, daily discomfort and disturbance confront them. Discomfort and disturbance can create the illusion of finality—until Jesus offers the alternative: the bread of life.

McKendree United Methodist Church serves a community meal for our displaced and unhoused neighbors every Tuesday. While we provide the food, the beauty of the experience is intentionally being with God's favorite people: the poor and society's disinherited. Without fail, every time I sit and break bread with our displaced neighbors, my eyes are opened to seeing the potential and possibilities of each human created. Breaking bread with one another can open our hearts to see the best in people. Family is formed when we sit and eat, knowing who provides the bread. Leaders who see discipleship as an essential element never waste a moment around a meal. Effective leaders use meals to start and embrace movements of intentional belonging and formational intimacy so that people can be strengthened by seeing the beauty in each other.

Time is a gift that you can never reclaim. Once it's gone, you must move on. Rev. Dr. Benjamin Mays, a mentor to Rev. Dr. Martin Luther King, wrote a poem entitled "I Have Only Just a Minute" that summarizes the value and urgency of time.

> *I have only just a minute,*
> *Only sixty seconds in it.*
> *Forced upon me, can't refuse it.*
> *Didn't seek it, didn't choose it.*
> *But it's up to me to use it.*
> *I must suffer if I lose it.*
> *Give account if I abuse it.*
> *Just a tiny little minute,*
> *but eternity is in it.*

As the disciples moved from the miracle of their abundant haul of fish—or future relationships—to the shore where Jesus greeted them with a meal, it took time to get to that moment. Miracles can happen in an instant, but most miracles happen over time. Jesus is compassionate and patient with his disciples and all humanity, and he calls the disciples back to recapture and reclaim alignment as a "follow me" people. Effective leaders understand the necessity of patience and empathy with people because everyone needs God's grace, a meal, a living wage, adequate housing, and enough clothing. True leaders create cultures of sacrifice, not cultures driven by survival-of-the-fittest.

After Jesus appears for the third time, maybe the disciples start to better understand and grasp the shift needed to participate in God's economy of abundance instead of prosperity. God has placed abundance on the Earth so that every person can share a sense of equity. Prosperity is when you take more than you need because you believe you are entitled to it, whether you earned it or not.

Earn all you can, save all you can, and give all you can are the three basic points of John Wesley's famous sermon entitled "The Use of Money." Wesley noted in 1789 that the Methodists of his day were ignoring the third part of his sermon. In fact, Wesley argued that the primary reason for the Methodist movement's ineffectiveness was the people's failure to give all they could. Wesley profoundly concluded, "If Methodists would give all they can, then all would have enough." Wesley's admonition for Methodists to give all they could was no pious rhetoric designed to increase contributions to the church budget. It was a plea for generosity and a plea for compassion for the poor and needy.

Jesus said it more simply, "It is better to give than to receive" (Acts 20:35 NIV). As a leader, Jesus teaches us to dive deeper into our understanding of sharing stories and our gifts to make our communities more vibrant and able to flourish in faith and action. Good leaders don't lose focus on the larger picture of community by focusing on their personal needs—*their* fish—but by broadening their perspective to the "us" and "we" instead of the "I" and "mine." Now, the third time, Jesus keeps inviting the disciples to "follow me." Every day is a new day to follow the leadership of Jesus. Giving is a discipleship and leadership trait. Giving releases us from greed!

> *I have given you an example that by working hard like this we should help the weak. We should remember the words that the Lord Jesus said, 'Giving gifts is more satisfying than receiving them.'*
>
> **Acts 20:35 (GOD'S WORD Translation)**

You can give money, time, and even presence. Several years ago, a group of us went on a mission trip to Matamoros, Mexico, to build a second floor of a Methodist church. We carried the cinder blocks from the first floor to the second floor and then laid them for the second floor. As we were talking with workers, someone from our team asked the local laborers how many hours a day they worked and what they were paid. Their answer: eight to ten hours a day for seven dollars a day. They made less than a dollar an hour! Needless to say, I was devastated by the reality of their cultural context. I started to appreciate why people are coming to America for better opportunities.

After being there one week, we packed our bags to leave for Nashville and decided collectively to leave all our clothing and everything we had, even our cash, to the church. So, we gave everything we brought, along with about twenty thousand dollars in medical and dental care. In that space, we felt the grace of God. From that place of grace, we gave because we witnessed Jesus!

Give yourself away. Jesus did! That's where discipleship and leadership emerge and end. We simply need to recapture and reclaim by reframing discipleship as a daily experience and expression of our faith wherever we gather.

Questions for Reflection

1. What about your discipleship practices need to be re-examined?

2. What's missing in your discipleship practices that you are willing to explore?

3. Can the way you understand discipleship be broadened to include specific ways people are shaped and formed?

CHAPTER EIGHT

Reinvesting in Cultures of Experimentation

By Stephen Handy

We are constantly learning and growing and changing. We are really an experiment. We are endeavoring to discover if a community of faith can exist purely for the good of others.
Erwin McManus

Laboratories for Experimentation

Remember that elementary experiment in science class? It was mandatory that everyone in the class participate, and the experiment determined a large portion of your final grade. The goal was to establish your hypothesis, a proposed idea offered on limited evidence with the hopes of a discovery. You then had to locate the necessary tools or instruments to help you or your team perform a worthwhile experiment. The goal wasn't to get it right but rather to immerse yourself into a process of informed learning.

Congregations and companies are the best places for experimentation! Why do I believe that statement? Think about where they are located and the reason for your organization's existence: to connect with people in the community. Experiments are leading us to something worth exploring, from grocery stores, restaurants, and coffee shops to school partnerships, barbershops, and beauty salons. Each week on Sunday, people in congregations become captive audiences. In essence, if disciples and leaders are always learning, most have built-in communities to learn from and about. Shifting from the other side means seeing your space or cultural context as a laboratory instead of static cultures and environments of people going through their weekly routines and rituals. What if leaders experienced their spaces of worship and employment as places for new learning, new adventures, and new perspectives?

Churches have some of the most underutilized spaces of any entity in America. Think about this space as an enormous laboratory through the lens of D3 where discernment, discovery, and deployment occurs. Seeing our spaces through the lens of a D3 perspective, D3 imagines discernment as the idea that God is already active in the neighborhood, embraces discovery as being openness to God's next "aha moment", and awaits deployment that ensures God will guide our next faithful step.

Typically, churches use their spaces on Sundays and

Wednesdays but very seldom are our buildings used Monday through Friday for community engagement opportunities and relationship-building. One of the positive moves of the pandemic was it shifted our attention away from the building as the gathering place so that we could reimagine and reinvest our efforts toward creativity and innovation in relation to people. We realized that buildings and the square footage of our spaces don't define the church—or any corporation, nonprofit, or governmental agency. Emerging from the pandemic allowed us to recalibrate our thinking to focus on connecting with people beyond the brick and mortar.

As I mentioned in a previous chapter, McKendree Church decided to "give" its building to the community. As a part of the process, we invited nonprofits to become missional partners in our common work or ministry of "Building hope through the love and grace of Jesus!" We soon discovered that many organizations—mostly nonprofits—were looking for partnerships to help build hope in the community. Our only non-negotiable was we needed to be given the opportunity to form (serving) relationships with their client base. All agreed that our missional engagements were extremely valuable to our joint and hope-filled efforts to create connections for human flourishing.

Meeting monthly to discuss what we are learning has

enriched and enhanced our understanding of the people we serve and those our missional partners serve. In the future, we plan to involve our missional partners in our visioning and planning sessions. Inviting others outside "our tribe" enhances our ability to "unlearn" and create new spaces for exploration and experimentation. Amazing shifts in thoughts and actions happen when we embrace the intersection of other sectors in our communities, neighborhoods, nonprofits, and governmental entities.

Experiments must be seen and shared so that others can observe and learn. Isaiah was a prophet who offered some encouraging words to a people who had failed and sinned constantly. God needed to announce a new way of being, thinking, and doing, all coming through the redemptive acts of Jesus Christ. Isaiah says:

> *"Do not remember the former things or consider the things of old. I am about to do a new thing; now it springs forth; do you not perceive it? I will make a way in the wilderness and rivers in the desert."*
>
> **Isaiah 43:18-19 (NRSVUE)**

At times, it doesn't feel that God is near, but God is all around us and evident in all of creation. Experimentation is one way for humanity to explore the next new thing. Genuine, resilient leaders are never satisfied with the norm or being stuck in neutral. Words describing the church as "mundane and mediocre" are not in the biblical text and are counter to the behavior of disciples who understand that life is a pilgrimage worth taking a risk as the Spirit leads us.

Unfortunately, for some time now, churches, nonprofits, and governmental leaders have stopped pursuing new places and stopped connecting with new people because of the polarization and paralysis that often comes over time from leadership in culture. We've lost our edge—or in the words of the Righteous Brothers, "That loving feeling." The pandemic didn't help generate a spirit of experimentation; it caused a spirit of retreating. Recently, though, I have found that the wind is blowing in a different direction away from the norm. Maybe we need to get back in the boat with Jesus and other leaders and cast our nets to the right or other side. Find two or three willing, eager, and compelled people to dream and launch into the depths of this emerging world.

Several months ago, a few colleagues gathered to process the future of leadership, community, and the church. We decided that intercultural competency and cultural intelligence were central to our experiments. Our experiment involved shifting the church from a stand-alone building where people came to us to meeting people where they gathered in their neighborhoods. Since coffee shops are popular gathering spaces, these are now often referred to as "third places," places beyond our churches or homes.

As discussed previously in Chapter 3, five generations are influencing our culture, workforce, and society today:

1. Silent Generation (born 1924-1945)
2. Baby Boomers (1946-1964)
3. Generation X (1965-1980)
4. Generation Y (1981-1996)
5. Generation Z (1997-2009)
6. Generation A (2010-2020)

From the beginning, we decided to invite people in their twenties, thirties, forties, fifties, and sixty-plus to be part of the core team and leverage the intercultural nature embedded in this group's DNA. Rules of engagement were established to ensure a culture of mutual respect and mutual accountability. Next, we identified a convenient, well-known location with a multicultural vibe, a multiethnic presence in the neighborhood, and where people wanted to invest in forming a community of belonging and intimacy. We are building the framework, so human and spiritual formation happens whenever we rediscover story-sharing around tables. After we confirmed all these crucial and connectional variables, defining the experiences and expectations was necessary. Our expectations were simple:

1. Create to honorable space for connecting people.
2. Create content that compels people "to be" with less "to do."
3. Ask self-awareness questions to better understand self.
4. Establish a missional engagement opportunity in the local community.

Shifting our thinking moved us to gather on a weeknight instead of Sunday morning, a data-driven idea that suggests people are spiritual but not religious, looking for community but not willing to attend a religious institution or church.

In our first gathering, we filled the coffee shop with diverse people representing four generations, all looking to experience the beloved community. Beginning with a welcome and a meal, people felt comfortable engaging in conversations and storytelling about life. Creating an environment of invitation is paramount to any community. Intentionally, we stayed away from church language but not from the words of Jesus, giving attention only to the four gospels. Never trying to convince people, we simply shared our stories about life, some good and some grounded in challenges. Everyone appreciated the honesty, humility, and grace extended—traits often missing in many churches. Unity in the body of Christ was evident but not forced. Amazingly, the participants felt open enough to start sharing from the depths of their hearts without fear of judgment. People returned to form deeper levels of community because, like Jesus, we lead with compassion, not condemnation. This is an example of shifting to the other side of the building and even church politics!

i4 Leadership

As you think about creating a culture of experimentation, consider the framework for leadership aligned with an i4 leadership model. After years of leading an Urban Cohort, I've developed a process to help leaders in every field become more like Jesus as an intercultural, competent leader. Intercultural, competent leaders have the ability and awareness to navigate and negotiate different cultural spaces. Here's a quick summary.

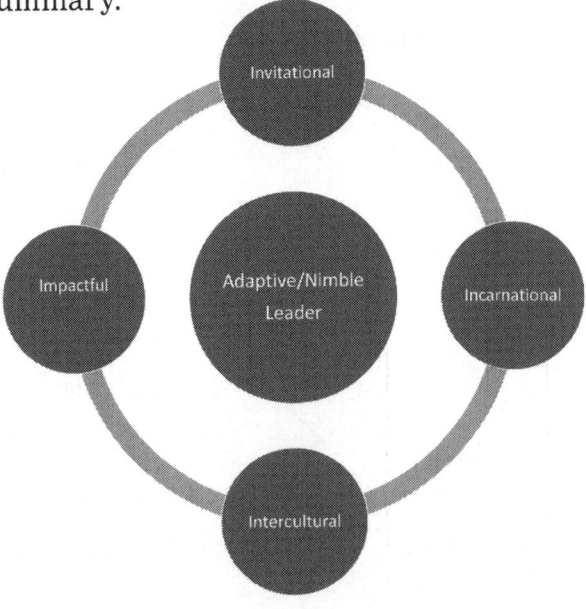

- ✓ **Invitational** – Being constantly clearer about your call! Realizing that in different seasons, we may need to reassess our call while identifying people we desire to invite on this journey of exploration and experimentation.

- ✓ **Incarnational** – Becoming the embodiment of Christ in your community. Assess the terrain by using Asset-Based Community Development tools. What do you know about your community and vice versa?

- ✓ **Intercultural** – Becoming an intercultural, competent leader, which is integrated into the DNA of disciples. Unfortunately, we have neglected this aspect of leadership as optional, unlike Jesus, who modeled intercultural behavior with non-Jews.

- ✓ **Impactful** – Creating experiments that will help reshape the culture into Christlikeness. We are often making disciples of culture instead of disciples of Christ.

Systems and processes are necessary and valuable for vital, resilient leadership to emerge.

Traditionally, leadership equipping is designed and developed within a classroom setting with one person presenting and providing information to be observed in a standard way. What if learning involved a shift from the classroom setting to community immersions? If this sounds foreign, think about how Jesus equipped the disciples, mostly through immersion in stories and parables. Immersions are places where the words of Jesus become real. The i4 leadership model establishes a culture of intercultural competency in the community where people do ministry and mission beyond one's own culture.

Think about how Jesus invited the disciples into a life of immersion experiences by simply using two words: "Follow Me!" There were no strategic plans or retreats to determine vision and mission statements because he *was* the demonstration that aligned the disciples to the mission of miracles, moments, and movements. No time was wasted on classroom bantering, board politics, or monocultural perspectives; transformation happened beyond the temple's walls in the marketplace where people were waiting. The marketplace was Jesus' laboratory. For example, the fishing expedition in John 21 was probably more of an experiment that Jesus invited the disciples to participate in after his resurrection. Leaders who shift their minds can more easily shift their bodies to the right or other side of their current reality.

One of the most dramatic leadership immersion experiences the disciples found themselves in was the feeding of the five thousand. Imagine being in an open field with thousands of people, not including women or children, who find themselves needing nourishment, something to eat after following Jesus as he performs miracles. Beyond the people gathered and those needing a basic meal, seemingly, there are no other elements for the experiment. Jesus opens the eyes of Philip, Andrew, and the other disciples to notice two elements for the experiment: five fish and two loaves of bread. Jesus takes the fish and bread, holds them up, blesses them, and the experiment becomes a miracle that feeds the five thousand-plus with twelve full baskets left over. Yes, the miracle provided not only enough to feed the multitude of people, but it secured enough food for the next experiment. Good leaders who participate in experiments are always looking for the next new learning, especially in seasons where change is constant and necessary.

Maintaining curiosity is essential to ongoing experiments. Curiosity is the force that drives innovation and creativity. Without curiosity coupled with compassion, the courageous paths to discovery, knowledge, and wisdom are simply distinct illusions. However, building a culture of experimentation involves more than just the traditional solo leader. Imagine the power of collective genius. Positioning and encouraging people in your church, nonprofit, company, or governmental agency to create experiments can be intimidating unless they are equipped and empowered. No one person should feel compelled to carry "the load" of leadership alone, but many don't see the collective model as an option. Burnout, exhaustion, fear, and doubt are expressions of working in the acceptable "solo leadership" role. We must shift to hear and see that God has an alternative way from what we are practicing. Cultures of experimentation are designed to disrupt and shift our disillusionment and discomfort to a place of miracles.

Several years ago, three friends from childhood who graduated from Tennessee State University decided that launching a business is better when it is established with a multi-person perspective and vision. Out of trust and friendship, a shared dream launched inside a garage in 2015. Slim & Husky's Pizza started as an experiment to shift the culture in urban and downtown communities. The company describes itself as a "fast casual, gourmet pizza joint as a way to serve unique pies and provide jobs to their neighborhood in North Nashville," and its motto is "Pizza.Art.Music." Claiming a heart for the underserved in the urban core, North Nashville became the first Slim & Husky's business plant. Slim & Husky's effectively uses food as an engagement tool to encourage and empower communities. What differentiates Slim & Husky's Pizza is this statement from one of the three partners, Derrick Moore: "We just want to be a part of this street as much as possible and continue to develop and have a footprint in this community."[31]

The experiment is working. From a humble location in North Nashville, Slim & Husky's now, as of 2023, has five locations in Nashville, one in Murfreesboro, one in Chattanooga, one in Memphis, Tennessee, and two in Atlanta, Georgia. As disciples and leaders, being able to discover and discern the other side of the current cultural reality is a game changer, a cultural disrupter, and a place where God is waiting for us to join the movement of God in the marketplace.

Another experiment is emerging. Our focus is clear. We have identified that when there is a core issue in the community where people need a solution, this is the best environment to launch an experiment. With the COVID pandemic wreaking havoc on people's emotional and mental conditions, three entities—churches, nonprofits, and state governments—are discussing what our response should be. In other words, we are contemplating how we can shift to the other side and deal with the current reality of mental and emotional trauma. We asked ourselves, what if all three entities were to work together at the intersection of faith and healing to counter the effects of trauma and educate

---

[31] http://slimandhuskys.com.

others not to see trauma as a flaw but as a protective mechanism instead? Resmaa Menakem, from his book, *My Grandmother's Hands*, comments on the evils of trauma on the body by suggesting:

> *The body is where we live. It's where we fear, hope, and react. It's where we construct and relax. And what the body most cares about are safety and survival. When something happens to the body that is too much, too fast, or too soon, it overwhelms the body and can create trauma.*[32]

As a result of our collective genius to equip frontline responders, we identified outcomes and decided to establish an academy for ongoing "equip" gatherings to cast hope to the other side. We hope this trauma-informed academy will equip responders who are deeply engaged with people experiencing trauma in our faith communities, nonprofits, and governmental agencies so that our cultures are hospitable, informed, creative, curious, and empowered to live faithfully into God's next move.

---

[32] Resmaa Menakem, *My Grandmother's Hands: Racialized Trauma and the Pathway to Mending Our Hearts and Bodies* (Central Recovery Press, September 19, 2017).

Questions for Reflection

1. What if leaders leaned into their community/culture and decided to disrupt the status quo?

2. Identify the gaps in your culture and develop solutions that could close those gaps and create cultural shifts.

3. What would it take for leaders in our churches, businesses, and nonprofits to reinvest in current cultures, participate in experimentation, and shift the community to reflect more diversity, inclusion, equity, and even more Christlikeness?

4. What components and elements do we need to take a step forward?

5. What stakeholders beyond our current groups, clients, and sectors need to be at the table, in the boat, in the sanctuary, or wherever people are hoping to find a faithful way forward?

6. What do we desire to learn so that our lives can be strengthened and positioned to assist with human flourishing?

Concluding Integration

Amid life challenges, hardships, and uncertainty, we must remember that we are designed by God as the *Imago Dei* (God's image) to participate in the Master's plan as creative agents with compelling thoughts and compassionate dancing. In the Garden of Eden, everything was present, and God was enough. Think about Eden as a place of possibilities and potential.

Humans are simply creative curators, actors/actresses on God's big stage of transformational movements.

This book offers our thoughts about developing an ongoing mindset shift while on this journey of restorative joy in Jesus! Today's times reflect a need for emerging, daring, and resilient leaders willing to see these critical and complex shifts as a spiritual practice of emergence. Our containers (our minds) are constantly recalibrating. Who are we recalibrating with daily?

Honestly, there is no better time to shift than now. While in crisis mode, perhaps we can better understand God's nudge to do something different, to "cast the net on the right side of the boat" for whatever the situation or circumstances are before us so that we can be, think, and do life magnificently.

We urge you to be bold, live compassionately, and stay curious in reassessing your personal and communal leadership principles. Make intentional, innovative space for what's coming, the shift needed, and the opportunities for renewal and reimagining of who and where we are in God's communities around the world. Take prudent risks while aligning the grace work that draws us closer to God. Be careful of assignment overload, where we become exhausted and nonresponsive because we are too busy and start to experience blessing deficiency.

Our book *Dare to Shift* is simply one of many ways to disrupt your conventional thinking and methods of "doing." We encourage you to apply these ideas, principles, and practices to create spaces of exploration and shift from a mindset of scarcity to fishing with a mindset of abundance. Let us create a movement of other-sidedness, or right-sidedness, with the kingdom settling on Earth as our goal! Shift to the right side and expect to experience God's abundance!

May the power of Christ be with you as you *SHIFT*!

Michael and Stephen

Other Books By
Market Square Publishing

FEED MY SHEEP

PREACHING GOD'S WORD

Emanuel Cleaver III

"Cleaver writes with deep conviction and years of experience, having seen the transformational power of preaching in the lives of thousands of hearers attending weekly in-person and online worship services. Feed My Sheep is an excellent resource for the seasoned preacher and a must-read for the new preacher."

Dr. Candace M. Lewis
President/Dean, Gammon Theological Seminary

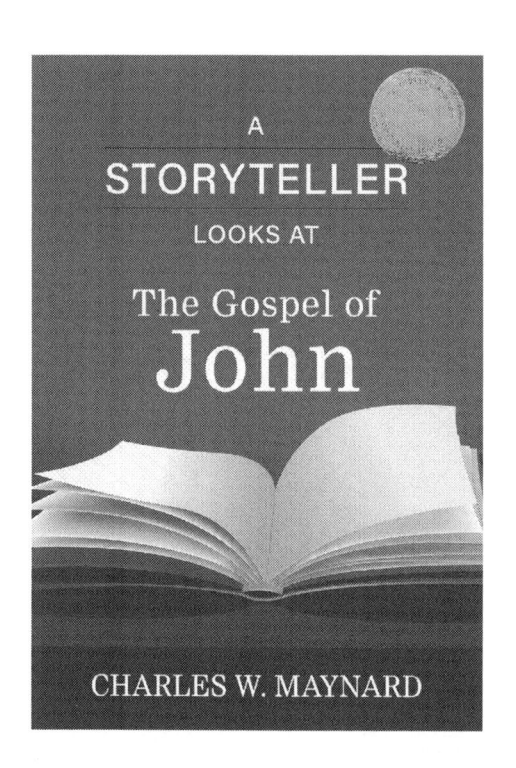

A
STORYTELLER
LOOKS AT
The Gospel of
John

CHARLES W. MAYNARD

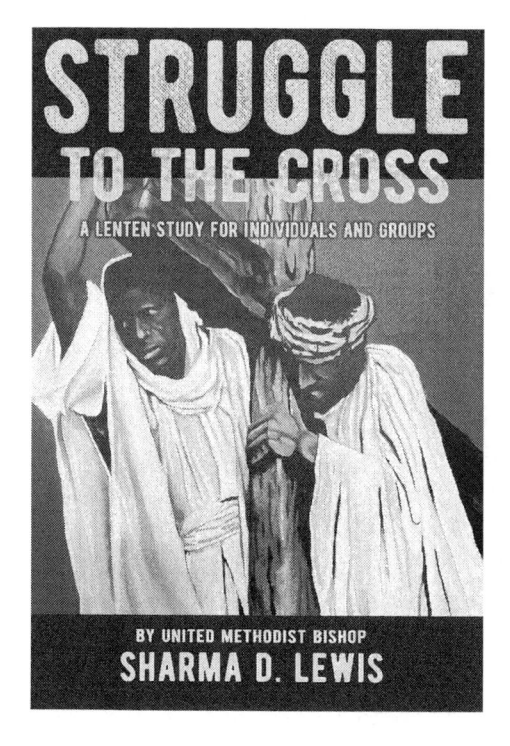

STRUGGLE
TO THE CROSS
A LENTEN STUDY FOR INDIVIDUALS AND GROUPS

BY UNITED METHODIST BISHOP
SHARMA D. LEWIS

Other Books By
Market Square Publishing

An Effective Approach to Cooperative Parishes
A Congregational Guide to Discernment and Implementation
Kay L. Kotan & Jason C. Stanley
Foreword by Blake Bradford
BONUS: AN EFFECTIVE APPROACH TO MISSIONAL HUBS

LIVE Faith SHOUT Hope LOVE One Another
A STUDY USING MATTHEW'S GOSPEL
M. Kathryn Armistead, PhD

FILLING THE VOID
Voices From the None Zone
Contributors:
Bradley Beeman, Jan Bolerjack, Lara Bolger, Kelly Dahlman-Oeth, Meredith Dodd, Emma Donohew, Kristin Joyner, Joseph D. Kim, Kah-Jin Jeffrey Kuan, Rich Lang, Lynne Pearson, Jenny Smith, Jeremy Smith, Heather Sparkman, Dave Wright, Karen Yokota Love
Compiled and Edited By Rev. Kristin Joyner & Lynne Pearson

forging a new path
REBEKAH SIMON-PETER
EMBRACING THE NEXT NORMAL
moving the church forward in a post-pandemic world

Made in the USA
Columbia, SC
06 April 2023